girls' night out

Celebrating

Women's Groups

Across America

girls' night out

TAMARA KREININ & BARBARA CAMENS

PHOTOGRAPHS BY LESLIE PARR

 CROWN PUBLISHERS • NEW YORK

Published by Crown Publishers, New York, New York. Member of the Crown Publishing Group, a division of Random House, Inc.

www.randomhouse.com

CROWN is a trademark and the Crown colophon is a registered trademark of Random House, Inc.

Printed in the United States of America

DESIGN BY ELINA D. NUDELMAN

Library of Congress Cataloging-in-Publication Data

Kreinin, Tamara.
    Girls' night out : celebrating women's groups across America / Tamara Kreinin and Barbara Camens.—1st ed.
        p. cm.
    1. Women—Societies and clubs. I. Camens, Barbara.
    II. Title.

HQ1885 .K74 2002
305.4'06—dc21   2002023383

ISBN 0-609-60867-3

10 9 8 7 6 5 4 3

First Edition

To my parents—

my mother, Marlaina, who passed along creativity, respect and passion for the written word, and an introduction to my first women's group, the sewing circle . . .

and my father, Max, who gave me the ability to embrace life and the stamina to get through it!

Together they instilled in me the desire for adventure, a sense of humor, and an openness to people and their stories.

—TAMARA

I dedicate this book to my parents, Arlene and Sam Camens, who made me believe that anything is possible. And to my beautiful sons, Jesse and Joshua, for their boundless joy and love. ". . . To the moon and back."

—BARBARA

acknowledgments

In writing this book our lives and life experience have intersected with those of hundreds of people who have inspired us, opened their homes to us, and given us support and encouragement.

We were first inspired in this project by our own women's group in Washington, D.C., that Barbara helped to start eighteen years ago. Our group was where we first met, and it was at a New Year's Eve celebration with many members of the group that we first decided to write this book. Our group gave us much food for thought—about relationships within a group, about what sustains a group or doesn't, and insight into how the girls' night out phenomenon has emerged in our society. Many of our group members also gave us a great deal of support. Though "once a member, always a member," the group of women that has been gathering around the dinner table lately includes Susan Burk, Susan Catler, Gail Davis, Mary Freeman, Joanne Hustead, Kathy King, Debra Lipson, and Sandy Moore. We send them much appreciation and affection. Special thanks also to Judi Minter, who first approached Barbara with the idea of starting a women's group almost two decades ago.

Tamara's various groups also gave us much inspiration—including Greater New Orleans Girls' Night Out and Chicks 'n' Flicks, as well as the Muses, who paint together in Washington, D.C.

Early on, several friends read our work, talked through ideas, helped us formulate our approach, and shared our excitement as we learned new stories of women's groups. These include the women of Tamara's family, Marlaina Kreinin, and her sisters, Elana Kreinin Markovitz and Miriam Kreinin Souccar (who might be considered Tamara's "mini-women's group" for a lifetime), Linda Gorby (whose clever use of words also helped on the book's title!), Emily Clark, and Sylvia Sterne.

We then met our fabulous agent, Gail Ross (thanks to Joanne, who made the connection) and immediately caught the excitement she shared for our book. Gail herself belongs to a women's group, the Shower Girls. She is a masterful editor, always sees the big picture, and is hugely creative and lots of fun. She is a wise woman indeed.

Gail led us to Emily Loose, our editor at Crown, who also immediately "got" our book and why what we had to say was important. Emily gave us great insight and ideas at the outset of the project and has done a terrific job of organizing our material in a way that makes sense to the reader. Again, our huge thanks.

Leslie Parr, our beloved and intrepid photographer, agreed to hit the road with us, camera equipment in tow, on nothing more than faith. Not only is Leslie a wonderful adventurer and risk-taker, she is a phenomenal photographer who immediately won the hearts and the trust of the many beautiful women she photographed. Leslie's humor and critical eye enhanced all our travels.

Our best stories surfaced by word of mouth. We asked everyone we met if they knew of any interesting women's groups—and many did! Among those who led us to groups are Penny Hughes, Sharon Barr, Andrea Johnson, Corrie Yackulic, Wendy Kahn, Jill Wrigley, Deborah Holtzer, Joy Dryfoos, Shelly Wood, Susan Burk, Priscilla Ebert, Antoinette Lopez, Beth Armstrong, Robyn Garnett, Joanne Hustead, La Donna Marshall (who also welcomed us so warmly to her Oklahoma home), Jenny Horowitz, Meg Scarlett, and Richard Friend.

We also had early help with publishing ideas from Bev Church, Susan Gillman, and Susan Tucker of the Newcomb Women's Center at Tulane University. Andrea Cipriani gave us our first beautiful images of the groups as we pitched our project to the publishing world.

Huge thanks go to the law firms of Zwerdling Paul and Barr and Camens, where we wrote and edited much of the book. (Special thanks to Wendy Kahn for taking photos and documenting the writing process, and Ingrid Coney and Donna Rainbolt for their technical support.) Not only did they give us space, they went above and beyond, making us feel welcome at all hours and cheering us on (even the men!). Tamara also did a good deal of writing in the home of Emily Clark and Ron Biava—there is nothing like a warm and nurturing space to make writing easier.

As we completed our draft manuscript, many people served as readers, providing invaluable feedback. We are hugely grateful to Sally Wessell Athmer, Jennifer Sosin, and Diana Pinckley for the time and care they devoted to our work.

Finally, each of us received special support and encouragement from family and friends, who kept us going and writing. Barbara sends special thanks to her two boys, Jesse and Joshua, to Peter, and to dear friends Joanne, Susan, Sandy, Sharon, David Cohen, Sally and her daughter Lauren, and Igor. Tamara thanks Elana and Miriam, David Souccar, Dennis, Raviv, and Netana Markovitz, her aunts Oshria and Marjorie, and other close friends, Linda Gorby, Jace Schinderman, Elissa Miller, Sacha Millstone, Emily Clark, Marly Sweeney, Sylvia Sterne, Nancy Aronson, and Ginger Besthoff, to name a few. We both feel very lucky to have these people in our lives. Finally, we feel lucky to have had each other through this process. We gave each other the encouragement, laughter, and sustenance that helped us write this book.

contents

preface

It crept up on us. Over the years, many years, it became clear. Tamara, the intrepid traveler, would pen "group" on her calendar and manipulate her work schedule to ensure that she could attend. In Barbara's busy life, juggling kids and career, group became the one get-out-of-the-house commitment to be honored consistently. When we would casually mention our groups to friends and colleagues, envy would cross their faces. They would beg, "Can we join?"

And when we first walked into the office of Gail Ross, our agent, to discuss this project, she immediately told us about the Shower Girls, her own women's group, and engaged us with their stories.

The evidence is undeniable. Women's groups matter.

Neither of us is a writer by profession. We were compelled to write *Girls' Night Out* because of our belief that women's groups are a great underground institution—even a central force—in many women's lives. We know that in our own lives, our women's groups have been both a priority and an anchor.

We are both in women's groups that have endured age and life experience. Barbara helped found a women's group in Washington, D.C., over seventeen years ago. Tamara was the first member of her women's group in New Orleans, Louisiana, to refuse to give up her spot when she moved away. She returns every month. When Tamara moved to Washington, the nicest "gift" she was given was an invitation to join Barbara's group. When her friends considered what would be most important to Tamara in celebrating her fortieth birthday, they remembered her long-standing desire to have both women's groups meet. They did, in New Orleans, for a surprise weekend of joyous celebration.

Since we first began talking about this book, we have constantly heard some variation of "You should write about my [mother's, sister's] group. They have been meeting over [coffee, mah-jongg, dinner] for years...." Though we have collected many stories, we have only scratched the surface. Through word of mouth alone, we have now found hundreds of groups, each with a unique and fascinating history. Women continue to seek us out to tell us their stories.

Writing this book has been a powerful and empowering experience. Women have opened up their homes and their lives to us, based on little more than an introductory phone call. They have allowed us to enter the intimacy of the moment. Their candor and trust have been remarkable. Women have shared the delights of their group experience; exposed the raw and the personal; told stories of conflict, disappointment, dislocation, and regret. They have joyfully shared their poignant rituals, their lessons learned, in the hopes of guiding and inspiring other women.

This project has moved us beyond the corners of our lives. We are sobered by the many groups that have faced illness and death, and feel fortunate that ours have not yet been touched. We are heartened by their enduring strength in the face of such adversity. Our fears of aging have been calmed by the many older women of significant beauty and grace we have encountered. We are astounded by the creativity, effort, and energy with which the groups have infused their time together.

Then there are the delightful differences that we uncover in these groups: the unique rituals; the innovative ways women structure their time together, or don't; the heartfelt stories that so personify the lives of American women across generations.

It was our belief from the beginning that the stories of *Girls' Night Out* would inspire other women. In fact, they already have. The process of creating this book has affected many of the groups we have met as well as our own. It has reunited groups with their founding members, as in the case of the Detroit Study Group, and caused women to reflect on the value and importance of their own group bonds, kindling renewed commitment among their members.

In Atlanta, we were brought to tears by one woman's confession. All of the other group members wanted to be a part of this project, but when she voiced reticence, her group stood behind her and immediately said they would decline the opportunity to participate. Their responsiveness gave her a whole new sense of belonging and erased her fears. The Company of Women, whose story is told in one of the following chapters, has taught us much.

Our encounters with other women's groups have enriched our own. Our love and respect for the women of our groups prompted this project. In turn, the experiences we have absorbed in writing this book have influenced our own group gatherings. Seventeen years after our Washington, D.C., group began, we introduced our first ritual—inspired by the stories of the women in this book. The lighting of candles and the recitation of our heritage has, for us, fostered a greater closeness, a centered feeling that has deepened our group connection. Our group continues to play with new approaches, inspired by our discoveries.

Writing this book in the middle of life has moved us, each of us. We have been forced to rethink our priorities, to examine what matters most. It has taken us beyond the everyday and has given us the opportunity to reflect, to think about changing our course and how one changes the course of life. In our own accomplishment and in the recounted achievements of other women, we see possibility.

Connections between women are often intense and complex; they can challenge our sense of equilibrium. We know the waxing and waning of commitment, the feelings of belonging and estrangement that can emerge within a women's group. In the end, commitment prevails. In the end, that is what is important—because we recognize that these relationships make our world both "wider and deeper."

This book is a tribute to the women of our groups, as well as those we have met across the country. As we note in the first chapter, women are forever being told to pay more attention to their families, their careers, their communities. We hope that this book will inspire women to pen "group" on their calendars and tend to their friendships with the women in their lives.

girls' night out

The GNO Phenomenon

It all began with the lucky dress. The women had been friends since the first week of college. They knew their friendship mattered; they just didn't realize how much. But when it came time to get married, it wasn't their mothers' wedding dresses that each chose to wear but Nancy's dress. Nancy was the first married among them.

A homemaker, a farmer, a teacher, a partner in a downtown Chicago law firm—their differences do not divide them; one woman's success shines on the other. "We realized at some point that we are like family, like sisters," Penny remarks.

Twenty years after they first met, the eight women resolved to formalize their connection—they became a women's group.

They make a regular commitment to each other, which they pencil monthly onto their calendars. They leave their homes, their husbands, their kids, and careers and get together with intention. They plan out-of-town adventures twice a year around Pam's farm schedule. They shop as a pack in New York City and drink margaritas together at the beach. They document their history with a scrapbook that travels with them.

They are present for each other at children's weddings, at parents' funerals. When one has a mastectomy, they are the first to know, and flood her with flowers. Their families come to acknowledge the group as a central force in each of the women's lives, an institution.

Standing in the middle of life this group of women now marvel at what they have created. "We know that we will gather together, that we can continue to count on each other, for the rest of our lives."

left to right: Mah-jongg Girls Jenny, Sam, Lauren, Sari, Marlow, Mara

This is the GNO phenomenon: women setting aside time just for each other.

As we have traveled across the United States, we have witnessed an explosive interest among women in making enduring and intimate connections with other women, not simply through individual friendships but through groups. While these groups have historical roots—the sewing circle, the quilting bee, the consciousness-raising "rap" group—a growing number of women are now seeking out and forging these connections. They are deeming them significant in their busy lives. Women's groups have become a phenomenon of our time.

The girls' night out spirit has swept into the fabric of our culture. The wild popularity of stories such as *Divine Secrets of the Ya-Ya Sisterhood* and *The Sweet Potato Queens' Book of Love* reflects this dynamic and evolving phenomenon. We hear all over the country about women, who would never seriously refer to themselves as girls, taking off an evening to have a "girls' night out."

Women's groups today range from the traditional to the virtual. Gen Xers form "grrl groups" or have cyber gatherings on the Internet. Others reinvent the sewing circle as "stitch 'n' bitch" groups or play mah-jongg with their girlfriends, embracing their mothers' passions. Thirty- and forty-year-olds return to their spiritual roots or find their creative voices, together. Fifty-year-olds continue the 1970s tradition of consciousness-raising, discover yoga circles, or confront issues of aging; eighty-year-old women gather in a local diner.

Of course, many a woman is joining a book group. But what is less obvious is that many of these women are seeking more personal connections than these groups readily provide. When asked, they often acknowledge this. They want a women's group. One group we met in New Orleans began as a traditional book group. Eight years later they still read books, but their focus is now largely on the personal. The women organize meals for the family of a member who is dealing with cancer; they take annual retreats to the beach.

And then there are the groups that don't realize they are groups, the unrecognized women's groups. The Bridgies of Needham, Massachusetts, spent a decade playing bridge before they admitted that they were more interested in sharing life than a deck of cards. There is also the woman in Minneapolis who spent years car-pooling with other women to work. When she left her job and her commute ended, she felt lost—and continued to ride to maintain the sense of connection. Many groups identify a "turning point," a moment at which the members realize the value and commitment behind their bonds. This happened to the woman riding to no job; she convinced the other women to start having regular dinners together.

Women's groups thrive in all walks of life. The women with the lucky dress hold their meetings on an Indiana farm. Prominent women, their faces familiar from prime-time television, make time for their ladies' lunch in Manhattan. A women's spirituality group in northern New Mexico meets in the "Moonlodge," a ceremonial space created by their own hand, inspired by the circular kivas of Pueblo Indians. Lurking in the halls of the Capitol building is a women's group of United States senators. Most women's groups we have met simply gather around the dining room table.

As we talked with women, we discovered commonalities in the face of difference. While women's groups are diverse, their members have a common desire to create sustained bonds with other women. Whether focused on sharing life or shared interests, these groups become an anchor and a priority for their members. They create a sense of belonging.

We live in an increasingly mobile society where family is often scattered. When our parents and siblings lived nearby, we could count on them to be present in our day-to-day lives. Women's groups can provide that sense of family. They mobilize energy and resources, and they lend extra hands. Prior generations of women could depend on institutions that often no longer endure: marriage, community, the proximity of family. Women's groups, through their enduring presence, offer a sense of rootedness, a common body of experience and knowledge, a sense of continuity. You can call a group member in the middle of the night when your child needs to go to the hospital. When you are dealing with a parent's death, your women's group will likely show up in your kitchen, organizing food and comfort. Facing an unnervingly significant birthday, your women's group can transform your regret into celebration.

Many groups persist through generations. In Northampton, Massachusetts, we found the Nineteenth-Century Club, which has been meeting to discuss books since October 23, 1894. We were also captivated by the Ladies' Mutual Improvement Association of Sandy Springs, Maryland, which considers itself to be the longest-running women's group in the United States. Begun in the late 1850s, many members were active in the Underground Railroad. Meetings begin with a reading of the minutes: "This is the one thousand eight hundred and eleventh meeting of the Ladies' Mutual Improvement Association...." The oldest member is 104 years old; she attends regularly.

Groups are also a means to connect with and celebrate the women of all generations in our lives. The simple recitation of their matrilineal heritage at the beginning of each evening together binds the Rosh Chodesh women of Philadelphia to their mothers, grandmothers, and great-grandmothers, in a way that is, for them, meaningful and important. One woman reflects, "Perhaps my daughter will someday sit with her women's group and recite my name as part of her matrilineal heritage. Perhaps the circle never ends." And sipping from their grandmothers' tea cups, the Tea Group of Boston observes, "No matter where our discussion begins, it always ends with our mothers."

Other connections are made through reminiscence. One woman we met in Washington, D.C., spoke of her discovery, upon her mother's death, of the journal her mother had kept for decades, recording the events of her women's group. This discovery not only rekindled the daughter's childhood memories of her mother's group but led her to connect with its few surviving members.

A women's group can also be a gift shared between mother and daughter.

Abby and her mother, Karin

For the women of a Seattle mother-daughter book group, their meetings are a way of sharing time and experience with their preteen daughters in an attempt to safeguard their daughters' self-esteem. As one member of the Tuesday Discussion Group in New Orleans poignantly explains, "This book group began in 1952. It was what my mother gave me when I married. We went together every month. Now that she is gone, I go alone."

WHAT DISTINGUISHES A WOMEN'S GROUP FROM OUR OTHER FEMALE FRIENDSHIPS?

Women's groups have a formality of purpose, an intentionality, overtly acknowledging the importance of the relationships they foster. The groups tend to have a constancy of membership over time, and are often strictly limited in number, with either implicit or explicit rules about new members and how they are selected. Whether they meet once a quarter for a weekend retreat, or every other Tuesday, the women commit seriously to set aside time for each other.

As a Bay Area group of women vowed at a recommitment ceremony held on their tenth anniversary together:

> We come together on a regular schedule with the intention of creating a structure, which allows us to nurture our goals, both together and individually. Our meetings are a retreat from the busyness of our lives, allowing us to step away from our daily responsibilities to a place that is both wider and deeper—a regular reminder that life is much bigger than our day-to-day concerns.

There is often an awareness among groups, perhaps unspoken, that "this is for life." We were awed by the simple longevity of many of the groups we have met. An eighty-five-year-old grandmother tells us about being a "latecomer" to her seventy-year-old Gals Club, formed when most of the women were students at Honey Creek High School in Terre Haute, Indiana. She joined in her twenties. Now at the end of their lives and mostly widowed, the women continue to meet weekly at a local cafeteria, as they are no longer strong enough to invite each other to their homes.

It is not difficult to understand the degree of commitment that often emerges within a women's group. There is a sense of unconditional love, and perhaps an ease of acceptance that we do not always encounter in our individual women's friendships. We have found that even those groups that gather originally around an activity or in the name of frivolity evolve to the more personal. In groups we go deeper in exploring our lives, our emotions, our relationships with each other, with our families, with the world. We expose more. The atmosphere of safety, the setting aside of time, and the group's intentional exploration of poignant issues all contribute to our willingness to be vulnerable. One woman from a Detroit study group recalls the moment when she realized that "these are the women I am closest to"; she was then compelled to confide, for the first time, the story of her search for the daughter she had given up for adoption more than a decade before.

Women tell us that groups can teach one especially important lesson: how to count on and to trust other women. As one woman from Atlanta reflects, "I associated female interaction with triviality, or worse. Negative things like jealousy. Backbiting. Competition." Groups allow some women, who otherwise might not easily develop female friendships, to back into such relationships. Another woman explains, "Many women have not been trustworthy in my life. So I often have one foot out the door. With these women, I am learning trust. They are teaching me about a sense of steadfastness and continuity which the rest of my life has lacked."

We find that women's groups can empower women at points in their lives when they feel the most vulnerable. In Los Angeles, a group of women who originally convened as a support group at a battered women's shelter now continue to meet and support one another as they successfully remake their lives. One woman in the Bay Area attributed to her group her courage to raise her daughter on her own. "I don't want to overstate things, but I never would have been able to raise a child by myself without this group. These women gave me courage, they allowed me to take the leap of faith."

Perhaps we are most vulnerable in our lives when our expectations are derailed. We are raised, for example, to believe that we will be married for life, that we will have a life partner on whom we can always depend. Women's groups counter the sense of devastation, isolation, and dislocation that may arise in the face of divorce or the breakup of a long-term relationship. As one woman from Massachusetts told us, "I was amazed at all of the support. These women accepted me without judgment. They made me realize that I wasn't alone and that people would approve of me." And even women in committed relationships may find dashed their expectations that their partner will meet their every emotional need. As one woman explains, her group helps her appreciate the person she comes home to at the end of the day because she doesn't expect everything from him.

Women's groups also bring intellectual empowerment. The elders of the Ladies' Mutual Improvement Association tell us that their group was founded "at a time when women had little access to learning." The responsibility of its members has not varied for over 150 years: each woman must arrive ready to discuss "a question and a comment." And the women of the Tuesday Discussion Group—the wives and widows of old New Orleans—have engaged their minds in an intellectual enclave of their own making, a salon of sorts. Many gained new confidence and a voice in their relationships with their husbands and their world. "It taught me to have a point of view," one woman remarks.

Even women of the "have it all" generation appreciate the stimulation a group can offer. One young mother confides her fears of social isolation and intellectual stagnation: "I need my group, so that I don't forget how to use my mind and speak to adults."

Women's groups are also a source of celebration and comfort. We find that groups will often honor and participate in life-cycle events as though they are family: weddings, bar and bat mitzvahs, birthdays, funerals. Their prominent

Phenomenal Ladies Pearl (left) and "Smiley"

role in marking life events reflects the high degree of respect women's groups command from members' families because of the important role they play in each woman's life.

Many women incorporate their own unique rituals into their group gatherings. These rituals call upon their shared history, and ultimately become tradition to be honored over time. For more than twenty years, seven women on Quadras Island, British Columbia, have begun their group meetings with a ritual reflective of their maritime culture. "We visualize the points on a compass—

east, west, south, north, and center." As a California group explains, their ritual has the ability to center the group's energy, to deepen its focus, to keep the women invested.

The group rituals we observed were wondrous. The Rosh Chodesh women engage in a ceremony that honors their matrilineal heritage and allows others to be brought "into the circle," symbolically extending their group to friends and family who are not physically present. The Bay Area group has a tradition of inviting all the women in attendance at a member's wedding to engage in their preceremony spiral dance, where they sing and circle joyfully around mother and bride.

Perhaps the most pervasive and central ritual among women's groups—their defining quality—is the ritual of conversation. Women's groups celebrate female conversation. Women process experience and emotion verbally, circling back in conversation, again and again, to develop and integrate their thoughts. They depend on good conversation to stay healthy and sane. The Tea Group celebrates this age-old female tradition of sharing life stories. Each time they meet, the women re-create an elaborate physical space—a tea room—where they drink from their grandmothers' teacups. As one member explains, "It is a sacred space. In our techno-fax modern age, women are desperate for a relaxing cup of tea and a stimulating conversation."

Women's groups encourage a unique freedom of expression. Our lives are complicated, often more complicated than the stereotypes allow, and so are our responses to them. Within the safety of a group, women are permitted to express less positive emotions, to be not simply "the good daughter," "the good mother," "the good wife," and to behave "badly"—that is, to be fully human. We will never forget the Network women of the Hudson River Valley in New York, women in their seventies who allow themselves to grouse a bit about the burdens and challenges of being a grandmother.

Women's groups are practical. They can keep individual female friendships alive in our increasingly frenetic culture. We have spoken to many women who count on their groups as the one reliable way to see friends when they are constantly on the road for business or otherwise immersed in work or family. Lessons can be learned from the standing Friday-night commitment of the Crew. Wherever they are traveling from, these Chicago women know they have a restaurant reservation and a seat at the table with their women friends.

Women's groups allow you to slide—at least for a while. We have all had times when commitments cause us to be less available to our women friends, generating guilt and bad feelings. When you are absent, women's groups can take the pressure off individual relationships and place them at less risk because other women can "fill in." When we know we have a friend in crisis who needs to process a painful experience, but we can't be there or take sufficient time, we are comforted in knowing that other group members will be there for her. Women's groups resolve many issues of reciprocity in this way.

Women's groups also help us with a "toxic" friend. We all have friends whom we love and value but who are difficult or needy. Within the larger whole, a group can share the burden and diffuse tensions that we would otherwise shoulder alone.

The structure of a group allows female friendships to weather life changes with less fear and more acceptance. Friendship often emerges from the security of sameness. In some fundamental way, it gives us confirmation of our choices, that we did it right. When our lives diverge, as we grow in different ways, friendships may be challenged. We have heard from many women that their divorce caused huge distress in individual friendships; friends may feel threatened and, in their own fear, be unable to provide the expected support. Though the groups themselves may experience the same upheaval, their promise of continuity holds the friendships together through the period of unease.

As Sandra from Atlanta wisely counsels, when you are feeling less than fully connected to other members of the group, you don't renege on your commitment, you honor it. "Sometimes you just show up."

In the end, the GNO phenomenon is about valuing female friendship, transforming friendship into institutions that are recognized and honored. We are forever being told to give more energy, more time, to our marriage, our career, our children, our community. Women's groups tell us to spend more time with our female friends.

GNO has become a phenomenon of our time. Women's groups are present, they are powerful, and they are enduring.

left to right: Pilar, Tamara, Audrey, Robin, Jennifer, Nisha, Sue Lin, Darlene, Lucy

Chicks 'n' Flicks

A braid of garlic hung on the front door, beckoning the Chicks to enter. As the women stepped into the darkened living room, the flicker of candlelight cast distorted shadows on the walls. A huge vase of red roses, barbed with forbidding thorns, sat on an antique sideboard. The dining table, set with a stark white cloth, was covered with black-and-white photographs of New Orleans cemeteries, the cemeteries where Vampire Lestat roamed.

Interview with a Vampire, based on the popular gothic novel by Anne Rice, was the night's flick.

That night the Chicks feasted on New Orleans fare and sank their teeth into a chocolate cake, iced blood red. During dinner the women discussed the appeal of vampires, the edge between evil and desire, between the grotesque and the beautiful. The conversation turned to their own desires. To seduction. Then back to serious film critique.

Chicks 'n' Flicks is a group of nine women in their thirties and forties, one just turned fifty, that gathers each month to discuss a movie. They select the film the month before, then, depending on their schedules, go to the movies together, in small groups or on their own. Over dinner, they assess. Thumbs up, thumbs down?

"As I recall, the idea for starting a women's group around movies took hold when I had just finished some big projects, an International Women's Film Festival, and producing a feature film," explains Robin, a video film producer and the group's founder. "I wanted a way to stay connected to film and connected to these women with whom I had worked so intensely. And because I wanted to expand my circle of friends, I invited some women who did not work in film. Women I wanted to get to know better."

The diverse group of women Robin brought together loved the idea. Many were involved with politics, public relations, video and news production, or other careers that entail heavy travel. They thought seeing a movie once a month and then convening to discuss it was a commitment they could manage, easier than a book group.

It worked. The first film, *House of Spirits*, was discussed on Robin's living-room floor in Adams Morgan, a multiethnic neighborhood just above downtown Washington, D.C. Eight years later, the group continues to meet. "Robin was the perfect person to begin this group, and to bring people together who didn't all know each other," explains Nisha. "She is the quintessential entertainer and friend. Everyone loves going to her home."

The evening always begins with snatches of conversation. The Chicks catch up on each other's lives, offer first impressions of the film, and recount stories from their recent travels. They sit down to dinner, and invariably Sue Lin focuses the conversation. "Okay, let's talk about the movie." The women discuss their reactions to the story line, the development of the characters, their thoughts about the cinematography and music. Nothing too intellectual, nothing too organized, perhaps even three conversations going at once, but lots of opinions, even from those who haven't managed to see the movie. "When you go to a movie," Darlene comments, "you lose yourself in another person's existence for two hours. This group allows you to prolong that experience. It's a total diversion."

The women often look for movies that will transport them far away from their workaday lives. *The Thomas Crown Affair* was one movie that provided just such sought-after escape. The gentleman-thief, portrayed by Pierce Brosnan, had enough money and style to get away with anything, including an art heist. The glamorous female insurance investigator, played by the enviably cool and beautiful Rene Russo, proved a worthy opponent. "These may not be characters we identified with," Jen says, "but, boy, were they characters we wanted to be. Even for a day." Robin adds wistfully, "I just wanted to look like that woman, with her sexy skirts and buttery leather jackets. I started working out at the gym just to get her triceps."

"It would be stressful and intimidating if the women expected rigorous film critique," offers Darlene. "But it's just so relaxed and comfortable. And sometimes it's just plain silly." A criminal prosecutor in a homicide unit, Darlene is the group's proud aficionado of trashy tabloids and the underworld.

The selection of the next month's movie is always done by consensus. The Chicks throw out ideas, naming the flicks they'd like to see, and providing mini reviews of those they have seen. Sue Lin pulls out the newspaper to be sure that no movie is overlooked. Each must be considered carefully. With all available information on the table, the narrowing down begins. If there is no obvious choice, the Chicks might take a vote. But if one woman lobbies hard for a particular film for whatever reason, the rest of the group relents. Unless, of course, that woman is Darlene.

"There was the time when we let Darlene pick," explains Jen, mischievously. "But that was before she sent us to the worst movie ever, *Heavenly Creatures.* Two young girls bludgeon their mother to death. We didn't let her vote for months."

In truth, the movie is often selected as much on the basis of the dinner that can be served as on the merits of the film. "We began with the simple concept of just seeing a movie and discussing it over dinner," explains Robin, "but then we started designing menus based on the movie. And then invitations, table settings, and other decorations." *Interview with a Vampire* was the first of such imaginative evenings.

Primary Colors, a comedy that explores the scandalous world of presidential politics, served as the perfect inspiration for another Chicks 'n' Flicks evening. Invitations were sent on "Bill and Hillary" postcards. Penned in red and blue ink, each card doled out an assignment: chicken wings to Sue Lin, potato salad to Jen, baked beans to Pilar, corn bread to Darlene. Tamara brought back a slab of ribs from a southern business trip; Robin fried ten pounds of chicken. And to top it off, Lucy baked an all-American apple pie. There is no Arkansas beer, so they settled for Dixie, from New Orleans. The patriotic party decor was easy—white paper tablecloth, blue-and-red paper plates. The Chicks unearthed political mementos from years past: hats, pins, and banners from many a campaign. Above the decked-out scene, American flags were flown.

Ever mindful of its members' hectic lives, the group makes sure that no one person has to carry the burden of cooking. Food assignments are always shared. That is, of course, unless the movie is an Indian film requiring a sumptuous Indian feast. Then Nisha or her mother is expected to produce. Born in India, both are fabulous cooks. "We quickly realized that we would see any Indian film, even a bad one, just so Nisha would cook for us," admits Lucy. She describes the night *Kama Sutra* was the chosen flick. "A whole table covered with Indian delicacies. Spicy curries, biryanis, samosas, and chutneys. And Nisha modeling several new saris she had just brought back from India."

Pilar, born in Panama, claims all Latin films. *Strawberries and Chocolate*, a sensual portrayal of an artist's life in modern-day Havana, was the first. Dinner was traditional *arroz con pollo*, roast chicken with rice. And, of course, there were strawberries and chocolate for dessert. Throughout the evening, the women discussed the film's arresting beauty, the cinematography, the city's pale light.

Eventually the discussion turned to politics. Everyone voiced an opinion about the political situation in Cuba, and Cuba's diplomatic relations with the United States.

Nine women. Nine opinions, all voiced with conviction but cloaked in good humor. The diversity of opinion is rooted in vastly different cultures and life experiences. The women come from circumstances of both privilege and deprivation. As they themselves recognize, the fusion of these cultures and disparities creates something rich and expansive.

The night we visit, the Chicks are meeting in Sue Lin's high-rise condominium in the Washington, D.C., neighborhood of Woodley Park. Five floors below, the city offers its chaotic take on life. Around the corner, on the urban thoroughfare of Connecticut Avenue, a hodgepodge of restaurants and shops reflects the distinctly international flavor

"This group is an equalizer. It's a great leveler, because we come from so many different backgrounds but find so much to respect and value in one another."

of the group itself. In a single city block, one can feast on the cuisines of Thailand, India, China, Italy, Japan, Lebanon, and Vietnam.

Sue Lin is a fourth-generation Hawaiian. The daughter of an obstetrician, she grew up in an affluent suburb of Philadelphia but spent many of her summers with her Chinese American relatives in Hawaii. She remains fully immersed in that culture. With her pale skin and jet black hair cropped stylishly short, there is something slightly imperial about her, a reserve born not of shyness but of self-possession.

For dinner Sue Lin serves a huge skillet of spicy chicken curry with basmati rice and green pigeon peas. The recipe is from Sue Lin's favorite cookbook, *The Crossroad of Cultures*. The dish's African, Indian, and Spanish influences are in honor of the night's film, *Butterfly*, set in the 1930s in post-Franco Spain.

Settling down to the dinner table among her guests, Sue Lin comments on the nature of the group's bond. "This group is an equalizer. It's a great leveler, because we come from so many different backgrounds but find so much to respect and value in one another."

Audrey, the first new member since the original group formed, exemplifies what Sue Lin means. "My background is so unusual," she explains. "I'm a Bud-Jew. I grew up Buddhist and Jewish. But in this group I feel accepted. I don't feel out of place." Audrey's mother is Japanese, and her father is German, a survivor of the Holocaust. "He went into hiding in Berlin as a teenager," Audrey recounts. "His family hid in the home of the midwife who had delivered him. Her husband was a high-ranking SS officer, but she agreed to hide my dad's family, at great personal risk. My dad was picked up by the SS just two days before the liberation of Germany. He was actually thrown in a cattle car destined for the death camps, but was released before he got there because the war was over."

Audrey's mother is from Taipei. Her parents met in Japan and settled in Seattle. They lived hand-to-mouth throughout Audrey's childhood, and the family shared one bathroom with all of the other tenants on the floor, down a dark, creepy hallway. Audrey's mother had great difficulty adjusting to life in the United States, and the family spoke mainly Japanese at home. Audrey recalls that some of the neighborhood kids taunted her family with racial slurs.

Other members of the group also come from immigrant families. Lucy's parents emigrated from Seoul when she was five years old, and her family spoke both Korean and English at home. "My father knew English because he had worked as a translator for the Anglican Church in Seoul," Lucy explains. "He worked for the bishop, so my father spoke perfect English, the Queen's English." Tamara's father spoke the Queen's English as well. He grew up under British rule in Palestine, before the Israeli War of Independence.

Perhaps the woman who's traveled the greatest cultural distance is the one

Robin, Lucy, and Pilar

raised closest to home. Darlene's parents have what she calls a mixed marriage, Catholic and fundamentalist Christian. They owned a sub shop and KFC called Al and Bob's Chicken and Subs in Bellingham, Washington. She recalls that when they finally managed to save three hundred dollars, they had an opportunity to invest in KFC stock. But instead they decided to buy a cow, which they named Enelrad. "That's Darlene, spelled backwards," she explains impishly. "I'm the first person in my family to go to college," she reflects. "My parents were living in a trailer when I was born. I had never known a rich person before I went off to law school."

These women are citizens of the world. While rooted in their unique cultures, they thrive on their group diversity, which fuels their friendships. The Chicks share a sense of dislocation; of being caught between cultures; of having a connection to many places, but not quite fitting into any one.

Tamara, daughter of an international trade economist, lived in five countries before leaving high school. She was once ridiculed for not knowing the name of the late-night talk show host who preceded Jay Leno. "I totally missed the phenomenon of Johnny Carson," she comments. She is grateful for all of her international adventures, but she sometimes has a hard time feeling anchored, fighting a sense of loneliness. She once described to a friend the sensation of entering an airplane as that of returning to the womb.

Pilar spent her childhood being constantly shuttled between the United States and Panama with her parents. "You learn to be resilient and flexible," she says, "but it can be difficult finding your place, your sense of identity."

Many of these women have stories of missing out on some cultural icon or historical reference that has forever branded them as less than authentic Americans. They have all traveled great distances to their current lives and have had to stitch together their own unique sense of culture. "When I was a child, I didn't understand Christmas or its traditions," recalls Audrey. "I was from this crazy Buddhist-Jewish home. I remember having heard something from the other kids in school about hanging stockings on Christmas Eve. I didn't know what I was supposed to do. I just took one of my socks and hung it, flat and empty, above my bed. And that's the way it stayed."

"Talk about feeling out of place," says Nisha with a laugh. "I've never told any of you this before, but Nisha's not my birth name. I changed my name in college, with a court order and everything. In India, there is this goofy tradition of naming babies with Western-sounding names. I know Indians named Sunny, Happy, Go-Go, Dimple, Simple, Twinkle. I hated my Indian birth name."

"Well, what is it?" the other women plead in unison.

Nisha's face reddens. "I'll tell you, I promise. But I can't just yet. I don't have the nerve. So, anyway, in high school I started taking surveys of popular names. And by college, I was introducing myself by a new name every week. I would come up to someone and introduce myself as Rita. And they'd look at me, all confused, and say, 'Wait, haven't I met you before? Didn't you say your name was Leslie?'"

"Come on, what was it? What was your name?" prods Darlene.

"All right, it was…it was…" Nisha drops her head and peers through a thick curtain of kohl black hair. "It was…Pinkie."

Everyone bursts out laughing.

"I'll never forget," Nisha continues, enjoying the levity around the table, "right after I finished school, I was handling my first press conference for a public relations client in New York. The client and I are walking down the street and all of a sudden I hear someone yelling from across the street, 'Pinkie, hey Pinkie!' It's a guy I hadn't seen since my first year in college. I'm doing my best to ignore him and just keep walking. But my client says, 'Isn't that guy calling you?' So I excuse myself, run across the street, and in one breathless moment tell the guy, 'I changed my name, I'm not Pinkie anymore, and I'd appreciate it if you wouldn't call me that!' So then I run back across the street and do my best to seem nonplused by the situation. But then my client looks at me quizzically and says, 'What was that guy calling you? Did he just call you Kinky?'"

The Chicks have spent many evenings speaking of the cultural tensions that inhabit their lives. Nisha was born in a small town in rural India and was left behind at the age of three with an aunt and uncle when her parents and brother first immigrated to the United States. She learned to be very independent. "But yet, I come from a very traditional family," she says. "My parents, my brother, are much more conservative, more observant of cultural traditions." Nisha works for a congressional committee on international relations and will soon be embarking on an HIV/AIDS fact-finding trip throughout South Asia. "I straddle two cultures," she observes. "When I am with my family, I am more traditional. But at work, I'm completely different. There's this tension that always exists within me. And I don't know how to resolve it. People call me Zelig. I am someone completely different in each new situation."

These tensions have often been the source of revealing discussions. One such conversation was provoked by the movie *Mississippi Masala,* which probed

Sue Lin, Jennifer, and Audrey

the challenges of a romance between an African American man and an Indian-born woman living in the South. That night, the group interrogated Nisha about the Indian tradition of arranged marriage and about her own intentions. Nisha admitted that she is torn between her strong connection to her Indian roots and her desire to make her own choices. She is proud of her independence, but is also keenly aware that at age thirty-two, she is already an old maid by Indian standards.

The international flavor of the women's lives has also sparked adventure. For a time, Nisha missed the group gatherings because she was living in Tbilisi, working for the Red Cross in the Caucasus. Robin and Jennifer went to visit. Loving the challenge of shopping and cooking in a foreign country, Robin took it upon herself to entertain all of Nisha's newfound Georgian friends. A Georgian cookbook became her most prized souvenir. So, *A Chef in Love*, set in the Republic of Georgia, became a must-see for the group. The food that the Chicks prepared was superb—roasted lamb, eggplant dressed with pomegranate seeds.

No doubt about it, the Chicks are global nomads. At a recent dinner, Robin asked matter-of-factly, "What do you do when you run out of space on your passport? I'm on the last page." Just as matter-of-factly Jen replied, "You get more pages added, of course."

But then the issue is where to get it done. "It's much better to be at a U.S. embassy in a foreign country," advises Nisha with authority. But which foreign country is ideal? With so many miles logged in their world travels, each Chick has her opinion.

Eavesdropping on conversations like these, one could think these women are international jet-setters with endless family fortunes. Or spies.

In fact, each of the Chicks is a hard-working, non-spying professional who has simply made world travel a priority, or part of her work. Obviously, the fact that none of them has children lends the Chicks the freedom to follow their wanderlust. But that dynamic may soon change. Several admit to a strong desire to have a family. "Yeah," says Robin thoughtfully, "I think the idea for this movie group first started in conversation with Liz, our long-absent member. Three babies later, Liz rarely gets to see a movie, let alone come to girls' group. There must be a message in there somewhere."

The commitment the women feel to the group transcends their many separations. They remain connected even when they are halfway around the world. Robin is currently on assignment managing a public-education campaign in the Republic of Georgia. Jen recounts with amusement, "The last time I came home from Chicks 'n' Flicks, the very next day I e-mailed Robin in Tbilisi, carefully describing the film, the food, the discussion, and everyone's gossip. Robin e-mailed back: 'Too late, Jen. I already got five e-mails from other Chicks, detailing the evening.'

"In some groups, women fall prey to groupthink. These women each have strong opinions and are not scared to voice them."

"In some groups, women fall prey to groupthink," observes Jen. "These women each have strong opinions and are not scared to voice them." But having met for the last several years, the women are now predictable in their uniqueness. The women fondly recount the evening when Robin identified their idiosyncracies so succinctly in a mini review of *The English Patient*, a film she recommended as having something for everyone. "All the Chicks will love it," she said. Standing over the women, she pointed. "For you, Lucy, there is romance. For Darlene, the adventurer, there is a sapper who deactivates bombs. And a plane crash in the desert. For Nisha and Jen, there is international intrigue. Sue Lin, for you there's fabulous cinematography. It's based in the Middle East, which you, Tamara, will love. And for you, Pilar, there is passion and heartbreak." The women were left smiling and speechless. Robin was so right.

The loyalty and devotion of these women to one another goes well beyond the scope of their group get togethers. If someone needs help of any kind, the others will be there. When one of the women is contemplating a career change, the others network for job opportunities. Despite her physical distance, Robin keeps sending job announcements from the Republic of Georgia, her favorite being a position based right there in Tbilisi. When one of the Chicks had a bad breakup, everyone was there to help. Several offered, "Come sleep at my house. We don't want you to spend the night alone." Another helped pack up the errant lover's personal items and place them where they belonged: on the back porch. And when Robin was in a panic about moving to Tbilisi, each Chick arrived to help pack. Of course, each had a different opinion: "Nisha told me to unpack five sweaters. Then Tamara arrived and told me to put them all back in."

Like a good Saturday matinee, Chicks 'n' Flicks has become a reliable pleasure for its members. Reflecting on the nature of their bond, Pilar mentions *How to Make an American Quilt*, a sentimental film about the friendships that often bind women for life. "The film was sappy, I know, but I loved it anyway. The women were connected through quilting the way we are connected through the movies."

The other Chicks will have none of this. Rolling her eyes, Jen counters, "Give me a break. We're a whole lot more like *Thelma and Louise*. Putting pedal to the floor, throwing caution to the wind, and taking each other for a furious ride."

Rosh Chodesh

"Ani D'vorah, bat Tema, bat Kayla, bat Tema. I am Deborah, daughter of Thelma, daughter of Carol, daughter of Tema." Deborah lights her candle and passes it to the woman seated beside her.

Elaine lights her candle with Deborah's flame. "Ani Elka, bat Rivka, bat Sima, bat Basha. I am Elaine, daughter of Ruth, daughter of Celia, daughter of Bessie. I just found that out." Elaine's face lights up over the recent discovery of her great-grandmother's name.

The women crowd together on couches and chairs pulled into a circle in Elaine's living room. They lean in toward a low table covered with a delicately embroidered cloth that Karen brought back from Israel. Each woman faces the clay candlestick she has crafted. In the center is a wooden box, from which the cloth and candlesticks have been taken. They call it their treasure chest. The women light their candles one by one as they recite their matrilineal heritage in Hebrew, and then in English. The circle is joined.

Quiet descends. What is important in life emerges. Everything else falls away. The women bring others into their circle by name and remembrance: a mother who died five years ago today; a father-in-law who is ill; a son who is preparing for a bar mitzvah. Deborah, with dark curls and a quiet dignity, speaks: "I want to bring in Talia, my daughter Talia, who created a ritual with

clockwise from lower left: Elaine, Karen, D'vorah, Deborah, Renie, Rochelle, Janis, Stacey, Linda, Lane, Valerie

her older sister on Thursday. Talia was inspired by Lag ba-Omer, the Jewish harvest holiday involving ritual offerings to the community. She built a campfire out of bits of construction paper, made a little speech, wrapped her blankie around herself, and offered up her pacifier." Karen interrupts to report, "Talia, my Talia, started walking."

These same eleven women have remained constant as a group for over a decade. Yet they have conceived this tradition to include others at their gatherings. And thus there are more souls than are present.

For this group of Philadelphia women, ritual is uniting. All Jewish, most married and in their forties, each with children, the women gather on the third Sunday of every month. Inspired by the practice of Rosh Chodesh—Jewish women coming together around the cycle of the moon—much of what they do in their meetings derives from their identity as Jews, but their bond has transcended those roots. "We've been through many life events together," observes D'vorah. "From deaths to births to bar mitzvahs. From sorrow to celebration."

Their group began with a celebration. "Our friendship with Janis brought us together," Karen explains. "Early on, we called Janis the hub." A dozen years ago, Janis invited eight friends to a thirty-fifth birthday affair at Bally's Spa in Atlantic City. At dinner, following an indulgent day in the sauna and hot tub, the women mused over their desire for a lasting connection with other women. Janis recalls, "I realized there was a void in my life which these women could fill. I wanted to add a dimension of meaning that I couldn't find anywhere else. A community for the long haul. A women's group." Deborah ventured, "Next gathering at my house," and so the Rosh Chodesh group was born.

At first, the group focused their gatherings on Jewish themes. While some of the women were active in their synagogues and in Jewish life, they all sought a greater connection between Judaism and women's spirituality. They met to explore their heritage and spiritual roots. The women brought new teachings each month to provoke discussion, some rooted deeply in tradition, others that examined the sacred in secular life.

"At first, we were studious in our approach," Stacy explains. "But over the course of about three years, the group evolved to a place of intimacy, tradition, and commitment. The group became a priority in our lives." In time, the women began talking about more personal issues—kids, community, marriage, and life dreams.

While there has never been a leader, the more interested and knowledge-able of the women in matters of Jewish study often take on the responsibility of preparing an exercise or religious teaching for that month's gathering. And the others generally don't mind if they do. Ironically, Val, who converted to Judaism as an adult, is among the most learned about and focused on Jewish study. She and D'vorah, who teaches at a Jewish preschool that she helped found, often take the lead. This dynamic has resulted, however, in a continuing tug in their meetings between the religious and the personal. "We are not just about Jewish study and we are not just a social group. So we are constantly retooling our approach," D'vorah explains.

"There is a continued tension between these two approaches," Renie elaborates, "but it is a positive tension, a creative tension which causes the group to constantly reflect on past experiences and to consider the transformative power of its future."

Each fall at an annual retreat, the women develop a plan for their activities for the upcoming months, a roadmap for the year. They will introduce new rituals or exercises intended to shift the focus from formal learning to personal exploration, or back again, depending on the wishes of the members. One year, for example, the group decided to present Jewish teachings only every other month; another year, they eliminated them altogether and concentrated only on more intimate issues. "We are a work in progress," concludes D'vorah.

The Rosh Chodesh group remains flexible in its approach. The right mix of formal study, personal support, and fun evolves according to the evolving needs of the women. One member, for example, who was initially less interested in personal exploration, the "touchy-feely stuff" as she thought of it, and who preferred to focus on formal Jewish study, encountered a series of challenging life experiences: the death of a parent, a bout with a serious illness. She is now among the most eager to explore her spirituality and inner psyche. "The support this group gave me in the midst of my hardest times in life has opened me up. I am much more willing to expose my own vulnerabilities and to attend to others."

> *"The support this group gave me in the midst of my hardest times in life has opened me up. I am much more willing to expose my own vulnerabilities and to attend to others."*

Content versus process, learning versus emotional support. "The compromise has felt the most positive," says Renie, "when we use our focus on Jewish ritual and learning to explore more personal aspects of our lives. In other words, we transform the religious into the personal."

The warm May evening we visit the group the women observe their version of Lag ba-Omer, an ancient Jewish harvest ritual. Deborah passed out interpretive materials derived from the Scriptures. The leaders had written references to female Biblical figures on the pages as a complement to the stories of the men otherwise featured there. The women devote the first hour of the evening to their study.

The traditional Lag ba-Omer ritual involves making an offering for the upkeep of the community. Extending this religious rite into their own lives, Deborah asks each woman to write down an offering, for the good of herself or for her community. The offerings are read out loud.

"I would like to offer myself the same nurturing I give others."

The group responds in chorus, "Make it so."

"I want to live a more poetic life. I work enough, give enough to my community." Another offering is placed in a basket passed among the members.

"Make it so."

"I commit to compassion and tempering judgment. I am thinking about what it means to be a compassionate leader at work."

"Make it so."

The ritual ends with a group offering, a commitment to more music and song.

"Make it so."

Honoring that commitment, Val distributes song sheets. "Hannah Sennish, a Hungarian resistance fighter, wrote this," she explains. "She was captured during World War II and tortured, but she never betrayed her cause." The women sing:

> *Oh God, my God*
> *I pray that these things never end.*
> *The sand and the sea*
> *The rush of the waters*
> *The crash of the heavens*
> *The prayer of the heart.*

Silence. From the depths of sorrow rises a resilient passion for life, and so, as a lesson of their faith, the Rosh Chodesh women embrace life.

For their annual retreat, the women head for the Jersey shore, in October, where they share a house on the beach for a weekend. Arriving by sunset on Friday, they all sit down to a Shabbat dinner. Val always brings the candles and the kiddush cup for the Jewish blessing over the wine. D'vorah brings a chal-

Valerie and Stacey

lah, a sweet braid of bread. For women so firmly rooted in family, these getaways allow them to step out of their roles as mothers and wives. They can be expansive with their thoughts.

Over the years, the weekends at the shore have developed a familiar rhythm. Saturday afternoons are devoted to a craft project. Many of the ritual items kept in the "treasure chest"—the physical symbols of the group—were made by their own hands. The clay holders in which their candles are placed, trimmed with bits of beach glass and shells, were made during a beach weekend. So too for the "shmatas," brightly painted table mats on which the candle sticks are positioned. These objects are uniquely valued because of the time spent together in creating them. The treasures pass with the chest from member to member each month so that the candle-lighting ritual can be repeated.

"Most of us are not artists," observes Renie. "So we have to fight our fears, our performance anxiety. But D'vorah leads us through." D'vorah, an artist, is a central force within the group, pushing the women through their discomfort.

Several years ago, the group created masks of plaster of Paris. Plunging their hands into sloppy batches of paste, gently molding the wet plaster on each other's faces, and then patiently waiting for the mess to dry, the women produced a series of lasting self-images. Janis, the massage therapist, made a cast of "those incredible healing hands." For another member, the project took on an even deeper meaning. Coming to terms with breast cancer, Deborah chose to create an image not of her face but of her altered breast. On the inside of the cast, she carefully glued a braid of satin ribbon—three delicate strands, intertwined—in the very spot where her breast tissue had been removed. Deborah recognizes that exercise as an important step toward healing, toward reclaiming her body as her own.

To give structure to their discussions at the retreat, the women hold a Rosh Chodesh meeting on Saturday night. There, they reflect at length on the group experience of the past year and brainstorm ideas for new traditions and new approaches. This is when much of the hard work of the group is done, in setting rules, establishing expectations, and deciding on goals.

The women choreograph "exercises" for the purpose of forging personal intimacy. One beach weekend they were each asked to share their life story, beginning with their births. "It went on for so long," Deborah recalls. "We all had so much to say. We just couldn't finish in a day." Recognizing the importance, the privilege in knowing each other's personal histories, not wanting to cut anyone short, the women continued telling their stories over the next several gatherings, deep into the winter.

The group also enjoys an element of whimsy. The women often play at the edges of mischief. And they play in a way that evokes a desire to reveal, to be vulnerable. During one evening of intimate revelry, they disclosed on slips of paper their fantasies of a former life. The papers were shuffled, and in turn each member was given a chance to match the fantasy with its author. The fantasies defied expectations. The less vocal, less verbally expressive among them revealed themselves to be evocative writers. Janis is a massage therapist and healer who devotes her energy to the comfort of others. Not one to call attention to herself, she surprised the women with her fantasy of a former life in the spotlight as a singer. Renie, who has "always felt most at peace swimming in the ocean," presented a poem she wrote entitled "Seal":

In a time before time
I dove into cool water
sleek and shiny black
head bobbing up for air
then down under wild waves
where fish were plentiful
I lay for endless days

on sun-soaked rocks
cubs and mate
breathing close and warm
sky and sea
holding forever

Another evening, the women brought with them journal writings from their adolescence. Their teenage writings, many in purple pen or florid cursive, were tossed into a pile. Again, they attempted to pair the writings with their authors. Poring over these intimate thoughts expressed so long ago, the women teased each other, gently.

Such exercises are always the highlight of the group's anniversaries, typically celebrated in a restaurant or with a potluck dinner. The women earn the right to choose a silly, inexpensive gift from a grab bag by matching correctly. Some are especially good at guessing, while others never get it right. "It is so endearing," remarks Deborah, "because we can always predict who will guess correctly right off the bat, and who will be left holding the bag. We know each other so well."

Lane, who teaches courses in group dynamics and has done a lot of group counseling, is often the source of these matching games. Photos of grandmothers. Baby pictures. The lyrics of a song you love. A dream you've had. This year, the anniversary gathering began at a health club and ended at a restaurant where the women were asked to share the title of their life story and its table of contents.

These games are not only a playful form of anniversary celebration but a means of candidly exploring personal histories and interior thoughts. Most memorable for all of them in that regard was the angel walk. Everyone stood in parallel lines. One by one, each woman walked slowly through the center, eyes closed. The others gently caressed her arms and face, whispering wonderful things about her. For the individual, it was a wondrously unnerving moment. And for the group, a loving act of validation, dispelling for each woman all uncertainty about how she is perceived and the things for which she is appreciated. "It was," as one member describes it, "a sweet and delicious experience. It was profound." Stacey reflects, "As if it did not occur in real time." Savoring her celestial turn, Deborah recalls that she walked through too quickly, that it was all over too quickly. She begged the group, "Can't I go through again?"

These experiences have much to say about trust. A safety net of enduring friendship allows the women to expose themselves, to reveal private corners of their lives not shared with the world. This kind of sharing is not without challenge. Some confidences have been revealed inappropriately to another friend or husband. But the response of the group has invariably been not to shut down out of fear or anger but to discuss the breach directly. Unlike other groups whose rules might be unspoken or nonexistent, this is a group that openly negotiates, that refines rules to work for each member.

"The quality of our communication is so valuable. We started out being very polite—but have worked hard to find ways to speak both truthfully and respectfully."

"The quality of our communication is so valuable," Stacey says. "We started out being very polite—but have worked hard to find ways to speak both truthfully and respectfully. We have tried not to shy away from conflict but to address difficult issues with care and honesty."

The Rosh Chodesh women also know how to support one another during challenging times. As Linda faced the stresses of defending her PhD thesis and missed several meetings, the rest of the women left a group message on her answering machine to offer encouragement. As Deborah grappled with the harsh reality of breast cancer, the others offered daily assistance. They engaged her children with art projects in her home so that she could just sit on her sofa and deal with her chemotherapy. They prepared meals for Deborah's family, provided child care, and carried Deborah emotionally through the travails of surgery.

"To feel held up by one another. That is one of the most important things about this group," says D'vorah. "It is a rock, a lifesaver." This sentiment is beautifully in keeping with the women's Jewish faith. There is no greater mitzvah—a good deed—than to care well for one another.

Devotion to Jewish ritual lends a comforting rhythm to their lives and gives structure to the group's year. The Jewish high holidays are celebrated in the fall. Rosh Hashanah, the Jewish New Year, and Yom Kippur, the holiest day of the Jewish year, mark a beginning. Renewal. From Rosh Hashanah to Yom Kippur are the ten days of awe—one's past acts are then inscribed in the Book of Judgment, which is sealed for the year on Yom Kippur. The Rosh Chodesh women begin these days in celebration, eating apples and honey to bring on a sweet New Year. Together they consider their lives, their sins, their treatment of one another, and their futures. Jews traditionally throw bread over their shoulder into a body of water as they cast off their sins. The Rosh Chodesh women write down what they wish to cast off for the New Year, set it aflame, and preserve the ashes between the pages of a journal kept by the group.

The Rosh Chodesh group is, by now, an institution in the lives of the women's families. There is a sense of respect shown by the families toward the group. "Our kids treat each other like cousins," explains Stacey. "We have come to celebrate the Jewish holidays together. And each Memorial Day and Labor Day, we have big family picnics."

Life passages are of great importance in the Jewish faith, and these women create their own rituals to celebrate the life passages of their children. When children are born, the women light candles and bless the babies. The blessings for daughters focus on the unique experience of womanhood and female friendship. The handwritten entries on the pages of their journal express their thoughts:

"I wish for you a friend like your mother has been to me."
"Less of a struggle living with your body than many women have."
"A centered presence and the serenity to maintain it."

The arrival of sons brings blessings that are equally heartfelt:

"Receptivity."
"Friends and connections."
"The ability to give and receive love."
"I have a feeling he will bless us."

At thirteen a Jewish child's transition to adulthood is marked through a bar mitzvah for a boy and a bat mitzvah for a girl. The group is part of this joyous rite of passage. "It all began at the bar mitzvah of Janis's son Koby, when she asked the group to come up to the bimah and sing," Renie explains. "We didn't have anything planned. We assumed we would all fall into a line. But, without thinking, we formed a circle, linking arms and facing one another. And then we sang the blessing we use to close each Rosh Chodesh meeting, 'Kol Ha Neshama.' We began together, and then broke into rounds. It was quite beautiful." So another tradition was begun.

Now, with the child's permission, the women sing to each bar or bat mitzvah celebrant, demonstrating respect for that child's growth and achievement. And the child, in turn, lights a candle for the group. The important place of the Rosh Chodesh women in these children's lives is thereby acknowledged.

Deborah and Elaine

At the time of her bat mitzvah, the women invited Janis's daughter, Michal, to attend a Rosh Chodesh gathering. Janis and Michal prepared a photographic collage of Michal's life. The women presented offerings, small gems, along with their blessings, which they wrote in the center of the collage. The offerings included a grandmother's jade heart pendant with the inscription "Go with your heart first," and a small straw box labeled "Be open and fill up." Michal placed the gifts in a silk pouch that she still keeps in her room. In return, Michal shared with the women her hope that their daughters will all enjoy becoming a woman as much as she did.

The Rosh Chodesh women archive their growing history, both graphically and in words. Lane faithfully documents each October retreat with a group photo. Laid side by side, the photographs of these women reveal their ever-unfolding stories: their pregnancies and births, their gentle aging, and their love for one another. And in the treasure chest is their journal, kept mostly by Rochelle and D'vorah. "They sit there at each meeting, at each retreat, and record things as they happen," observes Deborah. "We are so thankful because they have preserved our history."

Early on, the group determined not to allow new members, thinking such additions might come at the expense of the trust and common history they had developed. They also work hard not to let anyone go, a point they treat with lithe humor. "It is like that song," Renie says playfully. "You know—you can check out any time you like but you can never leave."

"Yeah," D'vorah replies, "we talk about who would get custody of the box. At this point, membership in the group is like a marriage. There is a sense of balance that we work to maintain." At different times, different members have felt that the group was not meeting their needs, or was getting in the way of their needs. The threat of someone's leaving has always provoked introspection and growth, for both the group and the individual. "We have given people permission to raise the issue of wanting to leave—we are that open and caring. At first it's frightening. But it opens up a dialogue." Sometimes, D'vorah observes, the group has modified its approach in order to keep everyone engaged. But at other times, where they felt it appropriate, the women have forced the individual to take more responsibility for the lack of connection. "We are all grown-ups," D'vorah explains. "We should be able to ask for the support we need rather than expecting others to dig it out of us. It's a complicated, layered dynamic that requires respect and sensitivity on both sides. But if we all take responsibility, it works."

There is now a profound sense within the group that it will endure. The women talk of pooling resources and buying a plot of land where they and their husbands may someday retire, as a community. They speak of growing old together. "We went to dinner recently to celebrate our group anniversary," remarks Janis, "and across the restaurant we saw a group of older women gathered together. We saw in them our own reflection."

The Rosh Chodesh women know they have built something lasting and important. Reflecting on that accomplishment, Deborah remarks, "I have a vision of my daughter seeing me in my women's group and understanding my profound connection to other women. It makes me so proud of what we have created. Perhaps someday my daughter will gather with other women, reciting her matrilineal heritage and including me in that history. Perhaps the circle will never end."

"I have a vision of my daughter seeing me in my women's group and understanding my profound connection to other women."

Regina, Sandra, Dena, Monifa

The Crew

As soon as I touch down on the runway," Regina says, "I turn on my cell phone and track down the other ladies. I say, 'It's Friday night. I'm home. Where are we having dinner?'" The Crew always meets late, around 9:00 or so. That gives Regina just enough time to land at O'Hare airport and make her way through the stubborn remains of rush hour traffic to the downtown Chicago restaurant where the rest of the Crew will be waiting. Their standing Friday-night dinner reservations give the members of the Crew a sense of constancy in lives that could otherwise feel disconnected.

The other women can never keep up with Regina's incessant work travels. "Regina is always e-mailing us in the middle of the week from God knows where," Sandra explains. "I always respond by saying, 'I know I'm in Chicago. But where are you?'"

"It doesn't matter where Regina has been, where she is traveling from. She always shows up on Friday night—poof—out of thin air," adds Dena with admiration. "Always ready to party with the Crew." "Party" in the best sense of the word—more laughter than overindulgence.

The Crew has assembled at a hot new restaurant. The bar and dining room are expansive, with a gray stone wall at the far end and an open kitchen filled with activity. The room is packed, and you can hardly hear yourself think. Dena, who is a producer for a syndicated TV talk show, *The Jenny Jones Show*, is on her cell phone, talking to a guest who taped an appearance on the show that day. Regina teasingly comments, "She's always got that phone plastered to her ear, answering calls, 'Jenny Jones, Jenny Jones.' We listen to it all night!"

Dena pulls the cell phone away from her mouth just long enough to stick her tongue out, and then continues her conversation, all corporate cool. The guest Dena is talking to is a self-avowed white separatist who appeared on the show to discuss the merits of his particular philosophy of racism. At the moment, he seems to be explaining to Dena that he likes her, well, notwithstanding that she is black. "I've decided—because of you—that I can like niggers," he offers magnanimously. Dena calmly ignores his obnoxious comment and with steely professionalism informs him that the show he was on should air sometime in late November.

The five women of the Crew—Dena, Regina, Mimi, Sandra, and Monifa—are hard-driving, high-achieving professionals, all in their thirties. Each endures the absurd demands of her long workweeks largely in anticipation of a glass of Chardonnay and the conversation they share on Friday nights. When they began meeting about five years ago, the Crew gathered only once a month. Now they meet just about every week, either for Friday-night dinner or for Sunday brunch. No matter what other commitments they juggle, they simply find the time.

The women poke fun that, among them, they can provide just about any form of service a person would need. Regina notes, "Sandra, our accountant, can do your taxes. Monifa, who is an engineer in telecommunications, can get you DSL. I'm in food product development, so I can provide any new food you want. And Maya"—Regina laughs—"well, Maya can get you subsidized housing!" Maya, nicknamed Mimi, is the director of grant development with the Chicago Housing Authority. "And Dena," Regina adds playfully, her voice rising, "she can always get you tickets for *The Jenny Jones Show*. But I'm always telling her, 'No way, Dena. My reputation is too important. I can't afford to get in the middle of a fight.'"

The women seated at the huge round table all point their fingers conspiratorially at Dena. Dena plays right into the joke. She tugs at her leopard-print cloche, straightens the collar on her matching dress, then lifts an elegant brow. Dena is flawlessly beautiful, a self-assured diva.

"You may not like it, ladies," Dena adds with a swagger, "but it's all about the Benjamin—the hundred-dollar bill. I'm going to make it big on the corporate scene. Someday I'm going to have a forty-eighth-floor penthouse on Lake Shore Drive. Just me and my rottweiler and lots of cats."

The mood among the women is "jumped up," as Dena would say. They are so engaged with one another that they never look beyond their own circle of faces in the restaurant. "It's like no one else is here," Dena explains.

"When we finally meet up with one another on Friday night, our personas change," Monifa says. "We can let down our guard for the first time all week. We all know how to 'do' corporate America. We know how to be well-spoken and competent and political. But with each other, we don't have to be. We use different words. It's a real comfort thing."

"When we finally meet up with one another on Friday night, our personas change. We can let down our guard for the first time all week."

"It's so easy for me to get completely engrossed in my job," admits Regina as she leans back in her chair. "Without the Crew, I would work all the time. When you are a single black woman in corporate America, you are always proving yourself. Even when you have proven yourself, you need to prove yourself again and again. This group keeps me balanced."

"It's true," echoes Sandra. "I coordinate corporate training seminars across the country. And, as you can imagine, things go wrong. Sometimes an instructor will be late. Or the materials won't arrive on time. And I'll catch hell for it. But when I come together with these women and listen to what they've been through, it gives me perspective. I can say to myself, 'It's only a job. Nobody died.'"

"I feed off of the Crew's energy," says Monifa. "By week's end I can feel worn down and I may not even want to talk about it. But just hanging with these women recharges my battery."

The women of the Crew talk often about how they negotiate two completely different spheres—the exciting, demanding world of largely white, male-dominated corporate America and the more familiar place they inhabit as successful black women, mirroring one another and looking back at their own reflection.

"Like, I was in a meeting this week," explains Regina. "Too much testosterone. As usual, I was the only female, let alone a black woman. Eleven white guys, one black guy, and one Indian. And me." The Crew members are often regaled by Regina's comic stories of the corporate boardroom, and they listen intently as she continues. "The vice president of marketing starts going around the room asking our opinions about whether we should relaunch a discontinued food product. Granulated bouillon. Very important stuff, ladies."

The women roll their eyes to the ceiling.

"Well, one after another these guys are saying, 'No, no, no. It doesn't make sense to invest in this product.' I'm thinking to myself, 'Yes, yes, it does. We should market this bouillon again, because it's convenient and there is a market demand for it.' But then I start asking myself, 'Should I say it? Should I say yes, when all these guys are saying no? When my boss says no?' Then I think, I'm different from all of these other people, so of course my opinion might be different. And when my boss gets to me, I say, 'Yes.'"

"Well," Regina continues, "then the president of marketing comes into the meeting. And he says, 'Yes, we should go for it, we should market this product again.' And the VP cautions, 'Well, only one person agrees with you.'

" 'That would be me,' I interrupt.

"And the whole time," Regina concludes with a throaty laugh, "I'm thinking to myself in that boardroom, 'I can't wait to tell the Crew about this.' "

Dena exclaims with great relish, "I always say, my 'sorors' have balls." The Crew all met as sorority sisters a decade ago at the University of Illinois at Champaign. They pledged to one of the few black sororities on campus, Alpha

Monifa and Dena

Kappa Alpha. "AKA was the first black sorority in America," Dena explains. "It began at Howard University in 1908."

"Of course, back then Dena would have been the only one who would have passed the Rule," Regina quickly adds. She goes on to explain the Brown Paper Bag Rule. "The story is told that for many years, until the 1960s, AKA pledges were limited to women whose skin was lighter than a brown paper bag. I know I never would have passed," Regina says, touching her hands to her face.

"We were thrown together in this sorority and we became close friends even though we are all such different people," Mimi observes. In her business suit, Mimi's demeanor is one of cool reserve. Her hair is pulled into a tight, low ponytail at the nape of her neck. "There were thirty-six thousand students on campus and less than one percent were black. In an environment like that you can't help but feel different. You look for other black faces."

"You assume that people who look like you will think like you, or at least that you have had the same experiences," Regina explains, "whether it's true or not. AKA felt like a safe place to all of us."

"The sorority didn't have a residential house on campus. None of the black sororities did," says Monifa. During their pledge period, all of the women of the Crew ended up living in Monifa's apartment, an efficiency. They were sleeping on top of each other. "We learned at that point to accept each other for who we are," she recalls. "And we have respected each other's differences ever since," adds Sandra.

"Regina is our people person," Dena explains. "She is always bringing people together. When she has a long morning commute, she'll get on her cell phone and start organizing, spreading the latest news on what's up and who is where."

"Regina sings into our voice mail. I save all the messages," Sandra adds. "And she sends e-mails to us all in capital letters with exclamation points."

True to form, Regina recalls, "Mimi lived in my dorm. She had an unapproachable look. But I approached her anyway. I wore her down until she became my friend." Regina then tells the story of the somber experience that cemented their friendship. "Freshman year, I had just gotten back from a weekend in Chicago when I got a call. My sister had been murdered. Mimi drove with me all the way back to Chicago in the driving rain. She said no more than two words, 'I'm sorry.' But that was enough. I played a gospel tape the whole way—Mimi hates gospel. I cried the whole way."

Dena continues, thinking back a decade or so to their undergraduate roots. "We all used to talk at AKA about what it was like to be such a distinct minority on such a huge college campus. I remember explaining to these women, 'I worked my ass off to get here. I always worry that people think I got here on a quota.' I told them about a professor who was worried about me being the only African American in her class. She asked if I was okay. I said, 'My question is, do you think I deserve to be here?'"

"It's funny," Regina points out. "All of the women in this group are diverse in thinking and in outlook. We have friends of every race and stripe—white friends, black friends, Asians, Indians, gays. But, in truth, I feel most comfortable in this group, with a bunch of women who look like me."

After graduation the women scattered, following divergent but ascending career paths. Regina went to Philadelphia; Mimi to Norfolk, Virginia; Dena to Columbus, Georgia. But they kept in touch. Dena, who strongly sensed the importance of these friendships, wrote letters to them all regularly. Over time, all of the women moved to Chicago, one by one. But their group identity was not deeply forged until Regina moved back in 1996, and took it upon herself to organize the Crew.

"We were all facing major life decisions," Regina explains. "I knew it would help me to talk with women facing similar issues. Strong, honest, open women who would not necessarily agree with me but who would not be judgmental."

The women thought hard about what type of commitment they could keep. Dining out on Friday nights seemed like just the right activity, and they all thought they could commit to once a month. "It was a commitment we were all willing to make." Dena smiles. "A commitment to eat."

"We take turns picking the restaurant and are always trying the latest, hippest joint. But when it's Mimi's turn, watch out," Regina warns.

"Yeah," Monifa continues. "One time, Mimi told us to all meet at a restaurant called Everest. We had never heard of it, and we had no idea what we were getting ourselves into."

Regina jumps in again, eager to complete the story. "Clue number one: valet parking. Clue number two: you don't have to pay for valet parking. Clue number three: you take the elevator to the fortieth floor, surrounded by a bunch of women in their little 'after-five' cocktail dresses."

"This is my family away from my family. We call or e-mail each other a few times a week."

The women were all coming straight from work. "But I came in khakis and a turtleneck sweater," recalls Sandra. "When I showed up and asked to be seated, the maître d' asked whether he could just send a message for me to Mimi's table."

"These women are all too proud to have left the restaurant," Regina observes. "I remember when I arrived I turned to Mimi and said coolly, 'Mimi, have you noticed that this is a fine dining experience?' We laughed through our lobster and our kir royales. But we laughed the hardest when we got the bill."

While the women obviously enjoyed their culinary adventures, they had come to savor something even more: their deepening friendship. The monthly sojourns became a weekly commitment.

"This is my family away from my family," Regina observes. "We call or e-mail each other a few times a week." "All except for Monifa," Sandra says. "She is elusive. We'll let her go a few days and if we don't hear from her, we have to track her down. If she doesn't return our calls, we call her boyfriend, Kevin, at work and say, 'What's going on with Monifa?'"

The balance between intimacy and respect for boundaries within this group is remarkable. They agree to disagree but are not argumentative. The women don't often give advice and try never to judge. "I remember when I told the Crew that I was separating from my husband," Dena recalls. "I told them that I didn't want to talk about it. They respected that. They didn't ask me any questions. They just accepted my decision."

Dena continues the story, her voice catching with emotion. "But these women looked out for me. They checked up on me. They made sure I wasn't alone. They knew I was having a hard time paying my bills. One night, Regina just left a check on my dresser without saying a word. We never talked about it."

Sandra is the only married member of the Crew, and she got married in college. "We all went home for Christmas break and got gold watches," Regina recalls with good humor. "Sandra went home and got a husband." Sandra and her husband and her two-year-old daughter, Jasmine, now live in the same apartment building as Regina. "We have a Saturday-morning tradition," Regina explains. "Sandra makes eggs, Jasmine throws them on the floor, and I clean them up."

Though the other women sometimes envy Sandra's happy family life, she frequently reminds them that there are two sides to the story. "They are always teasing me when they go off to play, saying, 'Goodbye, married woman with child.' But in truth, I do envy their freedom. They can do whatever they want. I need this. I need the Crew—to not be a wife and mom for a couple of hours."

The single women in the group tell the other side of the story. "Men, now

Regina and Sandra

there is something to cry about," Regina comments. "I've got some guy I met on my church group trip to Ghana, e-mailing me all the time. He must be sixty years old. He offers me airline tickets to come visit him. He calls me his chocolate drop. I'm always telling these ladies that if I don't show up for dinner some Friday night, it's probably because I've been kidnapped by that dirty old man."

Mimi fondly recalls the time Regina showed up with her list of thirty-seven criteria for the perfect man, her "ultimate mate criteria list." "What's the matter," Regina inquires, "do you think I set my standards too high? I realize I may be high maintenance—"

"And we realize why you are still single," Mimi retorts. "We spent a whole Friday evening laughing about that one." "If you don't set your standards high enough, you get in trouble," Regina responds. "We all know that from experience, don't we, ladies?" The others nod knowingly.

The Crew articulate with great humor a challenge many women face in relationships. "For so long, I wanted a relationship so badly," Regina relays, "and I ended up shacked up with a guy. Our relationship went downhill exponentially from day one. Every single night the guy wanted sex. Every night I got 'tapped.' And all I wanted to do was go to sleep. One night I even held Mimi hostage in my home. 'Don't go, Mimi, please,' I said. 'If you leave he'll want sex.' I was hanging on to her leg, pleading with her."

"I tell all of the single ladies of the Crew," Sandra explains with matrimonial wisdom, "this is what to expect: to get tapped every night. There is no such thing as 'I just want to go to sleep.' It's as if a guy thinks he will burst if he doesn't get it every night."

"Why not just say no?" Mimi asks, barely concealing her laughter.

"Because it will bring on way too big an argument," Sandra continues authoritatively. "And that takes too much time. It's faster just to lay back. You get more sleep."

Half bravado, half truth.

"Be careful what you ask for," Regina warns, "because now, no tapping, not ever.

"In all seriousness, we struggle a lot with the choices we have made in our lives," she says, "balancing the demands of career with the search for a fulfilling relationship."

The Crew then discuss another plight of successful women in the workplace: when the traditional balance of power between women and men tips the other way. "Sometimes, I swear, we look at ourselves and wonder if there is something wrong with us," Monifa comments. Dressed in a charcoal gray pullover, Monifa smoothes her conservative pageboy and continues in a quiet voice. "We are so confident and so competent out in the world but we have all had such problems getting our relationships right. Sometimes we ask ourselves, 'Why are we so driven to succeed? Is that the problem?'"

Regina has decided that if she isn't married by the time she's thirty-five, she will have a child on her own, and then adopt a second child when she's thirty-seven. "If that's what I need to do, that is what I will do. I grew up with a mom and a dad, but I know many women who do it alone," she says. "It involves sacrifice, I know. I realize I won't be able to travel. I may need a job that is less demanding, that pays less. But I will do with less. We are all used to having it all. But I can do it with a whole lot less. I know I can be a single parent and do it well."

The table goes quiet, and Dena's eyes glisten as she folds her hand over Regina's to give it a squeeze. "Would you really be a single parent when your children will have all of these aunties?" she says.

As the women finish dinner, they remember the night that Dena hosted the ladies for a slumber party. "The next morning," she recalls, "we all went over to IHOP for breakfast. The place was packed. We were seated at a long table with another party. We all started talking about life. About God and religion and men and marriage. Monifa was trying to decide whether to move in with her boyfriend, Kevin. We ended up crying over our pancakes. People were looking at us but we didn't care."

"When we are together," Mimi notes, "nothing else matters."

The women look up from the table for the first time all evening and realize that they have closed down the restaurant.

left to right: Lauren, Sari (in back), Marlow, Jenny, Sam (in back), Mara

The Mah-jongg Girls

In a New York City high-rise, a group of six Jewish women meets every other Tuesday night to play mah-jongg. From seven until midnight they gather at the table in rotating groups of four, the extras peeking over players' shoulders, egging them on. The mah-jongg tiles clink gently, persistently, as the women nosh on rugelah and chocolate babka. They smoke and drink Pinot Grigio. They matchmake like any good group of yentas.

But there is one surprise: they are all in their early twenties.

The babka is from Marlow's parents' bakery, and the mah-jongg set was donated by Mara's mom, Jamie. "Samantha's mom calls us the Oy Vey Sisters," Jenny says. Dressed all in black, Jenny is the very image of New York fashion.

"We are the very best of friends. We've been inseparable since we were kids," explains Mara, who is now a law student at New York University. "We spend all of our time together, but we decided that we should do something more organized."

Mara explains the origin of the group's meetings. Her mother started playing mah-jongg with a group of friends several years ago. "They played all day long sometimes, and I started tagging along, just absorbing the game. I decided that I'd get this group of girls to play. I wanted us to do something that we could do together fifty years from now when we are grandmas."

But Mara's friends weren't quite so enamored of the game. Despite all her prodding, the girls refused to learn until one weekend Marlow broke up with her longtime boyfriend. They rescued her to Sari's dad's house in the Hamptons to get away. Rain poured down all day and Mara realized she had a captive audience. "And I thought it would take Marlow's mind off of things."

The women agreed to learn the game, but really just as a kick—for its kitsch value. Mara picks up a mah-jongg tile, its red and green characters, vaguely oriental, betraying just a hint of retro-chic. "We all watched this mah-jongg video Lauren stumbled onto at work. And we called the mah-jongg hot line at the New York Mah-jongg League on West Fifty-seventh Street when we couldn't figure out the rules—there's a twenty-four-hour toll-free number."

"We think it's pretty funny that we play this game, a bunch of women in their early twenties. We always approach the game with irony," comments Sari. "But before long, the irony is lost and we're into it."

"Once we really began to understand the game, we got hooked," Mara adds. "It's challenging but also lots of fun. We try to make sure everyone wins, because we aren't really competitive." "But when you win, it's like winning an Oscar," Jenny says. "It's therapeutic. There is something about the noise, the click-click-click of tiles," Mara adds. "The tiles feel just right. We play with an older mah-jongg set my mother gave me. The edges of the tiles are worn smooth. A tile will fit perfectly in the palm of your hand."

"And when we plunge our hands in the middle, into the jumbled mass of tiles, well there is something wild and magical about it," Mara reflects.

These young women have discovered a secret shared by many women before them: mah-jongg is a remarkably intriguing and strangely sensual game.

The Mah-jongg Girls demonstrate that a regular, organized activity can bring a wonderfully reliable structure even to well-established friendships. And these women couldn't be closer. They first met as seven-year-olds at summer

left to right: Sari, Sam, Mara, Lauren, Marlow, Jenny

camp in the Adirondack state park on remote Raquette Lake. The camp was a spot to spend the summer far from the urban heat, a place of physical freedom.

These campers arrived in pairs. Mara and Marlow had known each other since kindergarten. "I remember, we had a 'show-and-tell' of our wood projects," Mara recalls, "and Marlow and I ended up fighting over whose project was whose, because we both had the same initials, M.A." They became fast friends. Mara tricked Marlow into going to Raquette Lake Camp by assuring her she could learn gymnastics there. "I told her they had the best gymnastics of any-where," recalls Mara, "which of course they didn't. But we had a blast."

Jenny and Sari were in a play group together in Great Neck, Long Island, when they were two. Their mothers became good friends, and so the girls did too. "I envied Sari's life," Jenny recalls. "She had a princess phone in her bed-room." Both Lauren and Samantha grew up in New York City, and they first met one another, as well as the others, at Raquette Lake in 1987. Sam was a year ahead. "I'm the old lady of this group. I'm the mom," she says. "I call these girls my chickens, or my bunnies." Samantha is all of twenty-five.

Most of the girls were in the same bunk at camp; there were two bunks for each age group. "They were all in the cool bunk, all except me," laments Jenny. "I was in the loser bunk."

"Yeah, but you were the coolest person in the loser bunk, Jenny," Mara con-soles her. "We did all the things you are supposed to do at camp," Samantha recalls. "It was not a competitive place, it was very friendship oriented. We learned to canoe on the lake and weave baskets. We'd sing campfire songs and dance in talent shows." But as Mara points out with good humor, "We were the camp rejects! We used to have 'color war' during Team Week. The teams would compete in all sorts of games and sports, and none of us ever got picked as team captain or even assistant." But not being picked brought them closer together as friends. They were part of what they called POMA, for "painters of murals anonymous." Those who weren't selected as team leaders or assistants during color war got to paint the mural for each team. "We spent every night hanging out in the dungeon under the drama hall, painting and laughing, while the team leaders stressed," recalls Jenny.

"We really grew up together at Raquette Lake," Lauren reflects. They spent hours in their bunks talking about boys and about their families. They would swap bunk gifts from their mothers' care packages, paint each other's fingernails and toenails and talk and talk. Many of the "firsts" in their lives happened during those camp summers. "Like our first kisses. There was a boys' camp right across the lake," Lauren continues. They smoked their first cigarettes together, and one summer they all got in trouble for smoking. "We even taught each other how to use a tampon," Jenny ventures.

"I remember Marlow asked me to shave her legs for the first time at Raquette Lake because she was so scared," Mara recalls.

"Those were some of the best times in our lives," Lauren muses. "We still tell stories about our camp adventures. The same old stories. But we never get tired of telling them." So fond are their memories that they all go back for a camp visit every summer. They serve as judges for the talent show, and float for hours in inner tubes on the lake. "I want my kids to go to Raquette Lake," Lauren admits. "I think we all do."

The Mah-jongg Girls found themselves forever bound by their lakeside high jinks, by the intimacies whispered between bunks in the dark. At summer's end, they were forced to return to their other lives, but they remained on some level inseparable all through elementary, junior high, and high school.

"Growing up on Long Island was so boring," Jenny says. "In high school there was nothing to do. So every weekend Sari and I would come into the city and sleep over at Sam's or Lauren's apartment."

Lauren was an only child. She was very close to her parents and was given a great deal of freedom and independence. "We found the lawlessness of Lauren's life remarkable," Sari says. "She could do anything she wanted, and she taught us all about the city. And about life.

"We would have so much fun exploring the city together. We'd do stupid things like dress up in funny clothes. We'd raid our mothers' closets and put on ponchos from the seventies or old ski jackets and hiking boots. Then we'd link arms and walk down Park Avenue together. We'd end up at some deli."

"We all made loads of friends at school. But somehow we all realized that no matter how many friends we'd make, these girls were the best."

"The one great thing about Jenny being a suburban kid," Lauren explains, "was her car. We love adventures with a car."

"For years I was the designated driver," Jenny says. "No one else drove. I would drive in from Long Island and pick up the girls in the city. We love road trips. We'd call each other up and say, 'Okay, it's Saturday. We need an out-of-borough experience.' And I'd drive all of these girls to the zoo, or to some orchard in the country to pick apples."

"But sometimes," Jenny continues, "we wouldn't go far. We'd just drive around the city. We'd drive up to a pretzel vendor, buy a bunch of hot pretzels and then just sit in the car for hours and talk."

When the Mah-jongg Girls scattered to college—to Tulane and Barnard, to Duke and University of Wisconsin at Madison—they found that absence did indeed make their hearts grow fonder. "We all made loads of friends at school," Sam explains. "But somehow we all realized that no matter how many friends we'd make, these girls were the best."

"We were constantly in touch while we were in school," Jenny recalls. "I'd duck out of the middle of class to send a group e-mail. We'd e-mail each other

Marlow and Jamie

incessantly. Whatever problems I was having, I'd pour my heart out to these girls." "When I fought with my boyfriend at college," Lauren says, "I talked with these women, long-distance, for hours and hours about it."

"Then, of course, we'd plan incredible adventures together for school breaks," Jenny continues. Samantha and Marlow went to school at Tulane in New Orleans, so for spring break of freshman year they all went to Mardi Gras. They would also make lots of plans for their time at home in New York. "We would go crazy with planning, two weeks before. One time we organized a six-way conference call in three time zones just to plan our break."

"And," Jenny concludes, "if we didn't go away together, if we weren't out with each other, we'd spend every night during break on the phone. Sometimes we'd sit on a conference call and just watch the same show on TV. We still do." *Sex and the City* is their current favorite.

"We are so close," Lauren observes, "there would never be an uncomfortable silence."

The girls knew that when they finished college they'd all return to careers in New York City, and they enjoyed the extra assurance that they would have each other's friendship as they embarked on new lives. Their ambitions have landed them in far-reaching corners of the communications world. Jenny is now an assistant segment producer for *Good Morning America*. Samantha is a fashion editor for *Vogue*. Lauren serves as a photography editor at *New York* magazine. And Sari, who wants to be a writer, is an apprentice to a professor at Barnard.

While the Mah-jongg Girls have thrived in the city, the homecoming has not always been easy. There are lonely moments of living on one's own. And, as sophisticated and savvy as these girls are, the stresses of fast-paced Manhattan careers sometimes take their toll. "We helped Samantha through her 'summer of tears,'" Sari recalls gently. "It was just hard for her, facing all of the changes in life. She was unhappy at work. She cried over everything. It was like a bloodletting. We were worried she would get dehydrated, she shed so many tears."

"We help each other when we are in tough spots, or are questioning things about our lives," Mara says. "When we discuss our boyfriends or the minutiae of our jobs," Mara adds, "we don't give each other bullshit answers. We speak the truth."

Sari adds, "We are so different, but we are so accepting of each other. We know each other's flaws."

"Like Jen is always getting yelled at for not listening. She has selective hearing," Mara says. "But Jenny was born under a lucky star. Things always come together for her."

"I rely on these women for advice on everything in my life, all the way from which shoes to wear up to major life decisions."

"And Sam likes to speak in grand pronouncements. Everything is so black and white in Samantha's eyes. We call her Sammy the bull," Mara continues affectionately. Mara dips a finger into a pot of clear lip gloss pulled from her bag, then passes it to Lauren seated next to her. The lip gloss will make it full circle. "And, of course, Lauren is our competitor. She's our social one." Lauren likes to organize everything, from fun to social action. Each year she organizes the group to raise money for the AIDS Walk.

"I'm the antisocial one," Sari admits with a shy smile. "If it weren't for these girls, I'd be a complete recluse."

Settling into their careers, still loving to scheme and plan with one another, the Mah-jongg Girls view life as one great big adventure. They host New Year's parties and invite three hundred of their closest friends. Birthday celebrations are extravagantly conceived, and they plan each event to match their different personalities. Samantha, the fashion editor, was treated to an evening steeped in glamour. "We picked her up in a stretch limousine, all dressed up in feather boas and tiaras. After a ride to the best sights in Manhattan, we took her to Chinatown for a Chinese banquet."

Mara, who digs the South, got a trip to the Cowgirl Hall of Fame, and all of the girls wore western shirts and cowboy hats. Lauren's love of Latin culture inspired an evening of dancing before a live salsa band. Sari, lover of children and children's literature, was given a bowling party with cupcakes, cone birthday hats, and goody bags.

And Jenny—wild, glamorous Jenny—was spirited to Vegas. "We all saved up our money for that one. Sam raided her own closet and had a 'tag sale' to raise money for the Las Vegas trip."

"Five dollars for a pair of Gucci sunglasses is still a good deal," Sam says in her own defense.

The Mah-jongg Girls may have come by their special friendship in part through inheritance. They are all very close to their mothers and grandmothers, both their own and one another's, and close friendships seem to run in their families. "We talk a lot about them," Jenny observes. "My grandmother is still best friends with her girlfriends from childhood. She shows me pictures of all of the things they've done together through their lives." "Our mothers are all our role models," Sam adds, "and close friends." "They taught us well," Jenny says. "Our mothers taught us how to survive life with good manners, and to respect ourselves. They taught us to value friendship with other women. They've supported what we've done with our mah-jongg group, and with our intense connection to one another. Our mothers are like the hands holding us up, together."

Reflecting on their closeness, Sari says, "We have lived our lives in each other's presence." Lauren comments playfully that "Sometimes we'll play Truth or Dare, but what's funny is that we know everything about each other, so it's all Dare."

"We are so very lucky to have each other," Jen adds. "I rely on these women for advice on everything in my life, from which shoes to wear up to major life decisions."

For all of their high-spirited revelry when they are together, the Mah-jongg Girls are quite serious about their importance to one another. "We are the center of our own little universe," Sari reflects. "When we envision our futures, there is a husband there for each of us, but he's always off fixing the television or something. These girls are in the picture, front and center. Some of our friends talk about 'girls' night out,'" she says, "but with us there is no 'girls' night out' because it's always girls' night."

Marcia, Mary Lou, Gail, Mary Lou (MLL), Suzie, Norma

The Bridgies

NEEDHAM, MASSACHUSETTS

W omen are raised to believe that their marriages will last for a lifetime. They grow up thinking that the one person they marry will meet their every need. But life often does not turn out that way.

It was Suzie who first broke the silence, in 1977. She told her bridge group that she was leaving her husband. She remembers, "I thought I was the only one. I thought everyone would disapprove." She had stopped going to bridge altogether at one point. "You had hidden yourself away," her longtime friend and bridge partner, Mary Lou, recalls, "you didn't want to see anyone." Suzie reflects that it was really only Mary Lou's prodding that got her out of the house again. "I kept making excuses not to go to bridge, and then finally Mary Lou said, 'You have to make a decision about going back.' It was hard, but somehow I did go back, and I was amazed at all the support I got, and not just from the women in this group, but from their husbands, too."

Mary Lou and Suzie grew up in Bath, New York. Both from Irish Catholic families, they met when they were ten. After college they decided they had seen enough of Bath. Young and single, they moved to Boston together. Each eventually married, settled in the same bedroom community, and had children. On the surface, Mary Lou and Suzie are a study in contrasts. Mary Lou's no-nonsense demeanor is a sharp counterpoint to Suzie's soft voice and dry sense of humor.

Despite their differences, they developed the kind of friendship that allows for challenging one another even at the tenderest of times.

Suzie, now a successful real estate broker, raised her three girls largely on her own. But she did not start out with that expectation. "Our identity was derived from our husbands in those days," she recalls. "I was Mrs. Joseph Clark. We were living sheltered suburban lives. Everything was defined for us."

And that is how bridge began. They were all young mothers, and bridge night was their only chance to go out regularly. A second Mary Lou, who goes by the nickname MLL, started holding bridge night at her house thirty-four years ago because her husband was out of town so often for work. "We craved adult company, so we started playing bridge. It was how we survived," recalls MLL. "When we first got together," Marcia remembers, "we used to dress up. Now, we take off our work clothes and put on something comfortable."

Sometimes it is the connections we make over the mundane in life that create the strongest ties. Through the easy routine of a twice-monthly bridge game, this group of women got to know one another. There was no initial pressure to be vulnerable or close. They just had to show up, join in the chit chat, and play.

They began as eight women, meeting every other Thursday. They always set up two playing tables, one in the living room and one in the dining room. Over time the women realized that whenever there was an intriguing conversation going on in one room, the players in the other room stopped to listen. Even so, the two-game arrangement continued for a decade, until one of the original eight dropped out.

For another five years the remaining seven women met and invited regular substitutes. Truth be told, however, they weren't focusing much on their bridge playing by that time. Suzie, who was shy and quiet when she joined the group but is now quite self-assured, remarks, "I can't believe the substitutes put up with us for that long." MLL's face warms with amusement as she recounts how all pretense of a bridge game finally ended. "The substitutes would get impatient. You couldn't get a substitute to listen to our chatter!" Suddenly, there is a chorus of all of the Bridgies: "And we didn't want them to." So one week the invitations to substitutes just stopped.

For a while they would still put up the bridge tables and take out the cards. "I don't know why, because we knew we wouldn't play," Norma recalls. "I guess we felt more comfortable having some sort of excuse for our gatherings." Finally, they stopped setting up altogether and just talked. But even all these years later, they are still the Bridgies. They still ask one another, "Who's having bridge next time?"

After the tables and cards were put away permanently, the women continued to meet every other week, for coffee and dessert. They loved to tell stories about their latest antics and the absurdities of day-to-day life. Everyone still loves to recall Suzie's story about the time when, early in her real estate career, she took a rather proper couple out house-hunting, only to look down to see that she was wearing two different shoes. "I almost fell down the stairs trying to back away," she says fondly, "but at least I sold the house."

Lighthearted conversation was the glue that initially sealed their bond, and that casual, upbeat style still characterizes them as a group. But these women have gone through their share of difficult personal times, including several divorces.

"We worked very hard at our marriages," Suzie comments. "Being in a good marriage with good children, that was your identity. We vaguely knew about the social upheaval going on in the world, about women's liberation. But we were insulated from all of that. We had children to raise. Women had a role, and that was to make it all work, even a bad marriage." Norma adds, "We probably stayed in marriages a lot longer then, it was easier to be in denial."

"It was only this group that helped me break out of my role," Suzie reminds her friends. "They accepted without judgment my decision to break up my home. It's funny, I didn't worry as much about the financial aspects of divorce, even though we were in dire financial straits." Suzie's father had died when she was an infant. Her mother was a journalist and supported and raised the family. It never really occurred to Suzie that she couldn't support her girls. "But," Suzie remembers, "I worried so much about telling other people and showing my face in public.

"It was that first Christmas I was alone," Suzie continues. "It was difficult socially to know what to do. Marcia called and invited me and my girls to spend Christmas with them. I felt like Marcia and her husband, Dick, really wanted us. I realized I would be acceptable."

Marcia, who just retired as a vice president of a large insurance company, reminds Suzie of how proud she was when Suzie first got her real estate license. "You were becoming Mrs. Suzie Clark, rather than Mrs. Joseph Clark."

Suzie's divorce made it easier for the other group members to face the truths of their marriages. "Suzie opened the door for me to be able to talk about my marriage and all the problems I had with my husband, Bill," Norma reflects. Suzie adds, with spunk in her voice, "Yeah, in the bathroom during Gail's daughter's wedding! I was stunned," Suzie recalls. "We stayed in that stall for forty minutes," Norma continues. "I guess I thought Suzie would understand because of her own divorce. My husband and I had been having problems for two or three years, but everyone knew Bill and liked him."

Talking about the divorce was terribly hard for Norma, because talking about anything personal was hard for her. She had never really had close women friends. For some time, Suzie was the only one she confided in. "I remember when I finally got up the courage to tell the rest of the women," Norma recalls. "We were down at MLL's house at the Cape. We had spent the whole weekend together and I still hadn't said a word. Finally, we were packing, it was the last hour we were there, and I just blurted out that I was leaving my husband." "Yeah," recalls Gail, "then Mary Lou said, 'I am too,' and I almost fell off the porch."

The women ended up staying longer that day. They talked and talked, startled by the revelation of two more disrupted homes. When they finally drove away, MLL remembers, "We were each in separate cars, but somehow it seemed like we were driving in one close huddle." That day was a turning point for the group, because they realized in a new way just how much support they could provide one another.

"This group gave me privacy, but they also never excluded me. I never thought they felt sorry for me; I felt they were with me."

As the women went through their divorces, they not only lent emotional support, but also gave lots of practical advice. Norma opened up in a profound new way, reporting all the steps she was going through with her lawyer and counselor. "I was one of those people who never shared," Norma admits, "but I shared all the details." The women all offered their opinions on difficult issues. "And," Suzie adds, "we acted like coaches for one another. We didn't know about support and about women's groups. It just happened."

"I realize I could have been more supportive," MLL says softly. "Especially with you, Suzie. I still have some guilt about it," she confesses, "about what more we could have done for you."

"But," Suzie reminds her, "no one knows what to do in these situations. If a spouse dies, people know what to say and how to act. With divorce, there are no rules and so often no one says anything. This group gave me privacy, but they also never excluded me. I never thought they felt sorry for me; I felt they were

Mary Lou and Suzie

with me. And that experience changed how my family deals with challenges. We developed a rule: 'When in doubt, say, When in doubt do.'"

In their thirty-four years together, these women have helped each other face many challenges, and have watched one another grow in many ways. When Marcia's husband, Dick, had open-heart surgery, the Bridgies took care of them both. They sent meals over for dinner every night. "In fact," remembers Marcia, "the Bridgies did more than our own families." When Dick felt better, he sent each of the women a rose, and after he had surgery again and they came through in similar style, he took them all out to dinner. "Dick will always love the Bridgies."

"Not long ago," Marcia says, "Dick told me that when he dies I can't move, because of the Bridgies." Marcia and Dick had been married for forty-four years, and when Dick got sick he started worrying about Marcia managing on her own and being lonely. He takes comfort in knowing that the Bridgies will be there. And the women themselves realize that while they may not grow old with their husbands as they had hoped, they have created a new kind of family.

"I would not move away because of this group," MLL says, as her eyes fill with tears. "The Bridgies are a part of my arm, I depend on them." MLL's husband, Bob, died six years ago after a difficult battle with cancer. Married for nearly forty years, things had always gone well for them. When MLL accompanied Bob to a hospital in Maryland for months of treatments, the Bridgies thought about what they would need away from home and sent care packages. MLL's favorite gift was a coffeepot and lots of coffee.

When Bob died everyone just showed up at MLL's home. She remembers, "It was great because it made my day easier, they all had me laughing. It's funny how these things teach us all. My children said they learned from the way the group just took charge. Now when a family member is in need no one is reticent, we all just show up."

The women have also helped one another take on new life roles. Among the Bridgies there is nothing but overwhelming pride in one another's accomplishments. When Marcia, who is a powerful presence and has always been at ease in the public spotlight, ran for commissioner of parks and recreation, all the women worked on her campaign. Suzie remembers watching Marcia get up in a public hall and speak in front of hundreds of people. "I looked at her and was astounded at her confidence and strength. That made such a big impression on me. It rubbed off on me." Each woman's success in her own endeavors gives the others a stronger sense of their own unique ability.

Norma is the new star of the group. She just graduated summa cum laude with a bachelor's degree in mechanical engineering, forty-one years after she graduated from high school. The group has given her a new nickname, "Summie." They are as proud of her as they would be of one of their children.

"When we were younger the differences mattered, we would point them out, I guess insecurity makes you do that. Now we care about the differences in a positive way. We admire and learn about each other's passions."

Norma, however, likes to point out that it was really only because of Gail that she went back to school. She had been working full-time as a designer because she needed to work after she left her husband. "Then," Gail adds, "two years after the divorce, Norma started dating Bill again, and that lasted four or five years. We were all so worried. It looked like Norma was going backwards. We would talk to her about it, gently. We would ask, 'Do you think those roses from Bill really make up for all he has done?'"

"I think it was sometime in there," Norma says, "that Gail got the brochure in the mail." Gail had received a flyer from Northeastern University and she gave it to Norma, planting the seed that she should go back to school. "I was sure she wouldn't do it," says Gail, "but she did." Norma smiles. "Before that, I didn't even have it in the back of my head to go back."

The women helped Norma quite a bit with her studies. "We all had to help," says Marcia with good humor. "I earned part of that degree." Norma excelled in science and math but hated some of the humanities courses, so she would bring her homework to bridge. "She'd bring the English worksheets, the music therapy, the psychology," Marcia laughs. "But it's Norma who can take my fridge apart and put it back together, fixed. We are absolutely different in innate personality, our interests, our likes, our dislikes."

"You know," Suzie adds, "when we were younger the differences mattered, we would point them out, I guess insecurity makes you do that. Now we care about the differences in a positive way. We admire and learn about each other's passions."

Suzie then pulls out a slip of paper and hands it to Norma, hinting that she finish her story. "Now tell the best part." Norma holds up the newspaper ad that the Bridgies placed in honor of her graduation:

We're Proud of You
Norma
June 17, 2000
The Bridgies

One of the most delightful transitions the women have gone through together is the release from their proper Yankee demeanors. They've allowed one another to become a good deal more risqué. Gail grins and remarks, "These women pulled me out of my own sense of propriety. We are so irreverent now that we are all older, and I just have to go along." "I didn't know you thought that," Suzie interjects playfully. "You sure complain enough about us and our behavior on our weekends away." Gail, full of New England reserve, defends herself. "Well, you have embarrassed me an awful lot, especially at our lake house in Sterling."

"Was it the skinny-dipping that caused us to lose our lake house privileges?" Norma wants to know. Gail laughs. "If I didn't do things like that with this group, where else would I do them?" Then Gail remarks on a serious note, "At this age you make acquaintances, but you don't make real friends like these."

When the Bridgies get together, they let down their guard and find new things to laugh at every time they meet. They laugh in the way that one does after years of history and knowing each other's idiosyncrasies. Despite the fact that everyone in this group was raised not to discuss sex, it has crept into their humor. Their conversations are spiked with off-color jokes that would surely make their families blush.

They all relish the time many years ago when, one weekend on Cape Cod, they were so hot that they decided to take off their bras. "We thought it was such a big deal!" remembers Mary Lou. "You have to know people really well to do things that would embarrass you."

Then there was the time that they all showed up at MLL's house in their pajamas, the night of her daughter's wedding. "I wore my best flannel," Suzie comments without cracking a smile. Pajama appearances have now become a common event. Marcia loves this tradition and remembers how it began. "It was after MLL's daughter's wedding. We all came back to my house for drinks. We had a few drinks, and it just evolved." Before they knew it, each woman was going home, changing into pajamas, and meeting back at MLL's house, all laughing so hard their sides hurt.

"We always laugh so hard together," Marcia says, "but that isn't all we do."

The Bridgies have eased each other through life's changes. Suzie recalls another transition. "My daughter Caroline was finishing graduate school in art and getting married. My other two daughters were leaving, and I was about to be on my own. My life as a mother was changing. The Bridgies were going away to Gail's summer house. That morning before we left, I woke up from a dream," Suzie explains, "and I had a poem in my head about the Bridgies, entitled 'We Are Seven.' I wrote it down. That was yet another point in my life when the Bridgies filled a void."

Suzie reflects on three decades of friendship. "These women taught me that everything isn't black and white. I am still learning—every time I am with this group. That not everyone's lives are the same. I learned not to live a role. I got outside myself, outside of that box. I stopped saying 'should.'"

Karen, Elizabeth, Caroline, Deborah, Sharon, Theresa

The Tea Group

Their ritual began with a reminiscence.

"I remember when I was a child, my mom would get together with her friends over coffee and cake. Everything else was put aside. I felt that these were sacred times for them. Now I understand why," recounts Liz, the founder of the Tea Group.

"I remember warm, delicious smells drifting from the oven, from my mother's baking. My brother and sister and I were always disappointed because my mother wouldn't allow us to taste what she had made; that was for her coffee group only. There was always a bit of mystery surrounding those group meetings."

Extending her mother's tradition to her own generation, Liz pours an arc of hot tea from the porcelain pot into the teacups raised by each of her friends. As always, the Tea Group women are gathered around a table, which is draped with an elegant cloth. Their teacups are family heirlooms, hand-painted and wonderfully mismatched one to the other. A fragrant cloud of steam—Earl Grey—moistens the air as the women take soothing sips, then balance the cups in their saucers.

"There is a rich physicality to it," says Karen as she wraps both hands around the warm base of her teacup. "The setting of a formal table, the tea ritual itself. The preparation and sharing of food. All of your senses are fully engaged. Something about the ritual causes you to let down your defenses."

The women of the Tea Group have been friends since they first met in art school eight years ago. The ritual of tea is the central gesture around which their conversations emerge. Bound by a passion for making art and for creating a community that rejects the competitive nature of the art world, these women have created a "feminine space, a women's environment," as they call it.

"We began as a result of need. We did not set out to start a women's group," explains Liz. The first tea was held in Liz's art studio at the Massachusetts College of Art (Mass Art) in Boston. It was February 1992 and the women were all graduate students there. Liz was enrolled in a multimedia program called SIM—the Studio for Interrelated Media. She had expressed her dissatisfaction to a male professor about the stifling nature of the classroom setting. "It was a very aggressive, competitive, male-oriented space. I felt like there was nowhere for me to speak."

Liz's professor challenged her to play directly with that frustration in her artwork. "He suggested that I invite other students into my studio to have a conversation. I remember thinking, Could this be a part of my art?" Liz set about creating her vision of an alternative space, one that was uniquely female. In a fit of inspiration, she transformed her studio into a Victorian tea salon. Liz laughs out loud at the extravagance of that initial effort.

"It looked like a movie set, a bit campy." She dummied up walls as a backdrop and covered them with lavender-striped wallpaper, embellished with a floral print. Then she hung her mother's white lace curtains above a mocked-up window frame. She decided she would ask each visitor to hang something on the Tea Room walls that related to his or her art or life: a personal artwork; a family memento; childhood photographs; intimate words. A round table, covered with a richly embroidered cloth and set with damask napkins, dominated the

Tea Room, and a vintage teapot and cups served as the visual and symbolic focal point of the salon. "It was a creative risk," says Liz. "It took on a life of its own."

With the salon completed, Liz extended to all of her classmates, men and women, an invitation to come for tea. Only women came. But that first tea embodied everything that the Tea Group was to become. "It was an inviting place where we could freely share our ideas. We found we simply didn't want to return to class," Liz recalls. "I think we realized from the start that we had created something powerful." That group continued to meet every week in Liz's studio for two hours over tea and breakfast.

"The Tea Group was so important to all of us. It is hard to communicate just how terrifying the whole experience was back then, being a woman artist with a particular creative focus, in the midst of that strict intellectual environment," Liz continues. "Even in the early 1990s, Mass Art was still traditional. It was an environment that was generally discriminating and unsupportive of women's work, though the dean and some of the faculty did really help us with our creative processes. Even so, the extra support from the group was huge. We found that we really needed each other."

From the beginning, the members of the Tea Group shared with one another their struggles to find their own creative voice. "I remember telling the Tea Group early on about an experience in my studio at school," recalls Karen. "I had completed an oil painting of a chair. It was a childhood memory, my grandfather's chair. The painting had real meaning for me. Well, one of my professors strode into my studio to review my work and, with one dismissive sniff, he decided that the painting must be hung upside-down. He liked it better as an abstract image. So there I was, left with a painting of my grandfather's chair, hung upside-down. How was I supposed to respond to that?" She shakes her head at the audacity, the outrage of it.

"There we were, a bunch of women artists creating works from our heart,"

Karen continues. "We were tapping into what mattered to us. Things like family and home and memory and personal loss. But it was all devalued. Those are the things we struggled with in our initial conversations as the Tea Group."

"These women understood exactly what I was feeling. They nurtured me and supported me in those tough creative choices."

Those early conversations had a transformative effect on the women, allowing them to feel more self-assured and comfortable about the kind of work they wanted to make. "I remember telling the Tea Group members about my turning point at school," Karen says. Recalling how another member of the group, Sharon, helped her recognize her true artistic interests, she continues. "I had been working in my studio, painting church interiors, grand spaces. The kind of important image I thought I was supposed to portray. But I was so stuck creatively. I remember Sharon came into my studio and we started to talk. She spoke to me about creating art that was important to me. Important to me, not to my professors. I remember, I sat down at the table and just began to sob. There was so much bottled up inside me."

That conversation with Sharon made Karen realize that she could be herself as an artist, and didn't need to paint grand images. "These women understood exactly

Caroline

what I was feeling," says Karen. "They nurtured me and supported me in those tough creative choices."

The Tea Group came to have an enormous impact on the women and their creative work. Caroline explains, "It was in the context of this group that I began to value influences on my work that I had previously minimized. Things like domesticity, women's work, family stories, and personal experiences."

"The women who ended up at the Tea Group needed to be there," observes Liz quietly.

Liz originally saw her role as a facilitator, so she scheduled the teas and suggested topics of discussion. For some teas, she assigned readings to stimulate conversation and to enhance their work. Inevitably, over time their conversation turned more personal. "Sometimes I would get frustrated because the conversation would stray. I thought we should be talking about 'capital A Art,'" Liz admits. "But I came to realize that what mattered most in our art was the personal stuff. It's what we were all about."

Many of the Tea Group members found themselves grappling with issues of loss. Terri, Liz, and Caroline all tragically lost loved ones. Terri's son died of an asthma attack and Liz's younger sister died in a car accident. And Caroline's very close friend Matt died of AIDS. As the women drew closer, they helped one another process the pain of those losses. "I remember telling these women that I couldn't paint anymore because it seemed too concrete," recalls Caroline. "The images on my canvas kept getting whiter and thinner. I was just overwhelmed by the sense of space left behind in my life by Matt's death. I only wanted to portray translucency and light. Well, the Tea Group got it. They supported me in expressing that sense of void, that emptiness, in my work."

Caroline stopped painting and began to construct a translucent maze out of tulle, the fabric wedding veils are made of. "In the end," she says, "the maze was large enough for several people to walk through at once. I decided to project slide images of bees' wings—a recurrent image in my dreams—into the tulle maze, larger and larger images as you wander through. It was a pretty ethereal piece. When I finished, I found that I had made a cocoon." Caroline pauses a moment in reflection. "I guess I was more hopeful than I had realized at the time."

The Tea Group conversations not only helped the women process their pain, they also helped them to understand how they could transform that emotion through their work. As Caroline explains, "I came to realize how the pain and introspection had given way to a prolific sense of creativity, of spirituality in my artwork."

As that year passed, the Tea Group gatherings generated a great deal of interest at school. Quite a few of their classmates began asking about joining, but the women decided they should limit their number. They attributed the success of the group to its intimate size. But they encouraged others to form their own Tea Groups.

Sensing the growing importance of their group history, Liz decided to document the group's meetings. "I kept Tea Notes of our conversations," she explains, "then documented the Tea Group ritual, the group dynamic, on videotape as a school project. People were a bit uncomfortable having their identities directly revealed, so I rigged a camera to the ceiling and shot the tape from above. A bird's-eye view. Just the table and the hands. The gesture of conversation."

That spring, before graduation, the school held a thesis exhibition, a group show of the graduating students' art. Realizing how much they had come to trust one another and to influence each other's works, the group decided to exhibit their works together, as the Tea Group. Liz wrote a thesis statement about the group and its impact on the members' art.

Spanning two full floors of a spacious, light-filled gallery in downtown Boston, the Tea Group exhibition was a critical success. While the individual works were vastly different in style, they were all somehow of a piece. The exhibit was a coherent and passionate embrace of the domestic, the personal, and the feminine, expressed in defiance of the prevailing aesthetic of intellectual abstraction.

Sharon displayed photo quilts that gave confessional witness to her family history. Karen had made oil paintings that presented modest, quiet images of childhood: an unmade bed bathed in sunlight, a bathroom glimpsed through a narrow doorway, her great-grandmother Matilda Donna's polka-dot dress. Through her life-size tulle maze, Caroline offered an ephemeral journey through loss to redemption. Drawing on her Jewish heritage, Deborah, the sculptor, used everyday objects as a visual metaphor for the Midrash, Jewish teachings. And Terri presented life-size portraits of underprivileged youth, iconic in their beauty. Liz's installation, *The Tree of Life*, involved five video monitors hung from the branches of a Japanese cherry tree, each monitor depicting an aspect of Liz's self: her relationship to the earth, the mind, the spirit, the body, and the family. "The tree bloomed gorgeously during the exhibition," Karen recalls. "As though it was meant to be."

Establishing a tradition for future shows, at the entrance to the exhibit the women carefully created a proper Tea Room. "We each made a piece of art around the tea," describes Karen. "My painting incorporated a poem with tea stains and leaves." Karen's mother's porcelain teapot, with its deeply stained and cracked interior, sat at the center of the round table. And at each of six place settings sat a teacup, passed down by a mother, a grandmother, or a great-grandmother to a Tea Group member. Liz's retro tea salon had become the group's icon.

"You wouldn't believe the reaction we got from other students," Liz recalls.

"All of a sudden we were accused of exclusionary tactics, of elitism. The Tea Group was branded as some sort of renegade women's group." The women were taken aback by the tone of the reactions. Caroline recalls, "We were floored. But it had a galvanizing effect on us."

The irony asserted itself. The Tea Group was born out of a sense of exclusion. Yet a powerful creative force ultimately arose from the commitment and support the women had shown for one another. And, unintentionally, the creative tables were turned.

Following graduation, the women feared that the group would falter, that they would lose their sense of artistic support. "You know the modern myth of the artist in the garret," adds Caroline. "All alone, with his torment and his sense of isolation. Well, through the Tea Group, we have tried to come up with another model." Meeting at Terri's home on Cape Cod shortly after their thesis show, the women decided that the Tea Group should continue, even though their meetings would have to be much less frequent.

The women now try to get together once a month, traveling to one or another member's home, and they continue to hold group exhibits of their work once a year. Several have settled around Boston, Deborah has moved to Maine, and Terri spends part of the year on Cape Cod and part in Florida. They've found that physical distance has actually added new dimensions to their relationships with one another. "We've gone to visit Deb in Maine a few times now," explains Caroline. "Or we'll convene the Tea Group in either Sharon's or Liz's studio in western Massachusetts. So now we take long road trips, all crammed in together for hours in the car. You know, we deal with traffic, we get cranky. But after being together for a couple hours, it feels really warm and secure. Like family."

"A family of choice," adds Liz. The group has evolved into an extended family of women supporting women. The Tea Group women speak often about being raised and inspired by the women in their own families. "My mother inspired me," Caroline reflects. "She, like her own mother, raised my sister and me largely on her own. I grew up at the feet of the Bridgies, my mother's women's group. They are all like surrogate mothers to me. There is a serendipity to it all. I went to graduate school to make art, but also seeking a similar sense of community. And I found the Tea Group."

"I have made so many pieces about my mother," Sharon confides. She is a photographer.

"One of Sharon's pieces is really amazing, really poignant," interrupts Caroline. "The Tea Group has discussed at length how it resonates for each of us. It is entitled 'I Always Thought I Would Be Just Like My Mother.'"

In the piece, three large images are mounted side by side: Sharon's mom, posed for her high school graduation picture in an elegant gown. Then Sharon's image in an identical pose, her features so reminiscent of her mother. And a final image of Sharon, staring defiantly at the camera, directly at the viewer. "Her look is so powerful, so unnerving," Caroline continues. "We've all talked about how that piece so honestly depicts our complicated bonds with our mothers. All that binds us and all that distances us from them."

The fact that the art of the Tea Group is so centrally focused on family reflects the strong legacy of these earlier generations of women. That influence also speaks to the complex views the Tea Group women hold of womanhood and home. Unlike many of their generation, these women do not hesitate to call themselves feminists and hold the full contours of the word. They can ably debate gender politics from the cozy warmth of the kitchen.

Several of the women have experienced difficulty having children. As women who place such emphasis on family, the thought of their own infertility threatened their core sense of identity. They recall teas where they laid aside all discussion of art and chose to confront their fear of infertility, and vent their

Elizabeth

feelings to one another. Anger at the manner in which fertility treatments had suddenly invaded their bedrooms and consumed their every thought. They also shared their anxiety that if they were not to become mothers, who were they to become as they moved through life?

"We've shared a lot of our sorrow with one another, especially during those long car rides to one another's homes," recalls Karen. "I will never forget one of the teas at Sharon's house several years ago. She had announced earlier that she was pregnant, and we were all so overjoyed for her. Then she had a miscarriage. Sharon talked at that Tea Group gathering about coming to terms with the fact that she may never be a mother."

"I told the group that I was an only child, and the family archivist. I was the keeper of the family photographs," says Sharon. "I come from a family of photographers. The family photos are very important to all of us—they are the visual proof of who we are. I told the Tea Group that day that I realized I may never have a child, and that there would be no one to pass the archives on to. The thought was extremely painful to me." Karen quietly adds, "It was not a very dry tea."

Each of the women who struggled with conceiving a child has now been blessed, each with a daughter. Sharon has Emma, Deb has Hannah, and Karen, Eva; Caroline has Alice, named for her great-great-grandmother. That four daughters were born to this group of women all in one year seems, to each of them, less a coincidence than a story unfolding, a story they somehow share.

Despite life change and distance, their story continues to unfold in the art they exhibit together. "There is still a coherence to our work which really comes through in our group exhibits. Our work continues to contain threads of the same material, even though we are not all artists of the same medium," says Liz. And, by joining resources, they have achieved greater success. "We benefit from each other's connections in the art world," interjects Caroline. "We share the hard work of obtaining a commitment from a gallery, generating publicity, and installing the exhibit."

"Perhaps our collective effort has helped us to be consistently productive," Caroline continues. "We have found that we are more prolific. And our joint efforts have helped us to achieve in a way we might not have as individuals."

In 1996, the women decided to explore the idea of their connectedness through the medium of quilt making. "We collaborated on the Tea Quilt, which we now hang at all of our group shows," explains Karen. "It was a tough project. We each worked on our own squares and none of them matched. We ended up snapping at each other as we stitched them together. But the quilt is beautiful. It's a physical expression of the connections between us and our work, an artifact of our relationship." It is also a means of honoring an art form that is uniquely female, and that has brought American women together in intimate conversation for centuries. "It's a place for our works to live together in a way that we do not," adds Liz, "a way to continue our conversation."

> *"Women think and communicate in a fluid, circular manner. We like to visit, and revisit, and revisit again interior thought. And the very process of sharing those thoughts is what makes women feel connected and engaged."*

The Tea Group women are now exploring ways of creating a larger community of women artists while retaining the intimacy of their own group. They have developed a Web site, which documents their continuing group history and their artwork. With the click of a mouse, you can download photographs of the Tea Room, the Tea Quilt, and the group's latest works, at www.theteagroup.com. And they are experimenting with the notion of a global tea—a Tea Room in cyberspace where women can connect through audio and video links. "We would allow women to log on from around the world," explains Liz, "and participate in a global conversation."

The Tea Group exalts the timeless phenomenon of women gathering intimately with other women. Its brilliance lies in its recognition of the profound beauty and value of that process. It elevates female conversation to an art form. "It seems to me," says Caroline, "that women think and communicate in a fluid, circular manner. We like to visit, and revisit, and revisit again interior thought. And the very process of sharing those thoughts is what makes women feel connected and engaged. It is an essential part of our lives."

The importance of female conversation is something that our mothers and grandmothers understood, at least intuitively, as they gathered in the warm refuge of their kitchens over their baking, their sewing, their quilt making, their cup of tea. This is the wisdom of another era that Liz and the Tea Group women now embrace.

front row, from left: Ina, Rosalind, Fran, Robin; *back row, from left:* Brenda, Marianne, Linda C., Gail, Marly, Tamara

(GNO)2: Greater New Orleans Girls' Night Out

The land in west Louisiana is flat and wide. Any member of (GNO)2 will tell you. You see the sky reflected on the fields of the rice farms when they are flooded for seeding. In March, when we visit, the air is light and fresh, not yet burdened with humidity.

Most of these thirteen women have been making the trip together from New Orleans to this wide-open country once a year for more than a decade, to spend a weekend at the family home of one of the group, Linda. They know the three-hour drive so well that they long ago gave up the maps Linda used to draw for them. Heading west on I-10 from New Orleans following the Mississippi River, each year they stop on Government Street in Baton Rouge for Lebanese food—Sirop's, the best in the state. Then it's on through the Atchafalaya Basin and into Cajun country—Lafayette, Breaux Bridge, St. Martinville. The billboards on the way advertise a Cajun dance party, known as a fais-do-do. It's a road trip, so Marly will be sure to drive through McDonald's for french fries and Diet Coke, a must for her friend Tamara. Leaving behind the assault of the interstate, the women drive on. The roads narrow. They come upon the farmland.

As they turn off the last back road onto the long driveway of the home, called Thornwell, the gravel crunches and spits out from under their tires. The large, graceful oaks that once arched overhead are now gone, destroyed by a hurricane. Just beyond the row of newly planted saplings sits a weathered horse barn of peckie cypress, long abandoned. The white, two-story farmhouse finally comes into view.

Thornwell. Linda grew up with this farm, homesteaded by her great-grandfather. Her daddy was the president of the local bank, and her uncle was the mayor of her hometown of Jennings, Louisiana. Daddy keeps the place up now mostly for the girls to visit, making annual improvements just for them. "Each year when we return, I wonder if my daddy will still be here next year," Linda confesses. He is ninety-one. To the women of the group, it seems inconceivable that someday he and Thornwell might not be waiting for all of them.

But this year, at least, Daddy is fine and the farmhouse is ready for their arrival. It is Friday afternoon, and as each car approaches, the passengers peer up the drive to see who has beat them. They have just arrived, but already they're worried that they've missed out. "No one better have taken my bed," proclaims Brenda, the self-anointed princess of (GNO)2.

(GNO)2—Greater New Orleans Girls' Night Out. Named for their beloved city, a city of decadence and celebration, this group of thirteen women enjoys a huge appreciation for life. Hanging with this group requires a thick skin, a large sense of humor, and a desire for intense emotional connection. "You have to be tough, to be able to banter, or you can't survive this group," observes Judy, a prominent New Orleans psychologist. "It is like a big family where everyone just cuts in." Affectionately dubbed the Southern Savages by one member, (GNO)2 is a rousing, slightly bawdy celebration of female bonding.

(GNO)2 was started more than a dozen years ago when, in hot pursuit of female friendship, each of five founders invited two close friends to lunch. Questions were prepared to help break the ice and to allow the women to learn a bit about each other: Who was most recently married? Who had traveled the farthest distance to lunch? Each woman left with a corny gift scavenged from the hosts' homes. Rosalind received a single place mat for being married the longest. Linda got an Ace bandage for having the largest chest. And all the guests were invited to join the group.

The next event was a slumber party, with pajamas required, even though no one spent the night. Linda, a therapist specializing in issues of child abuse, scored the highest points for silliness. She arrived dressed in flannel pj's, with pink sponge curlers in her hair and Clearasil dots scattered across her forehead. During the evening, the women discussed "serious" matters: their first kiss, their first love, the number of times they had been married. "Obviously," says Brenda, shaking her silky, champagne-tinted pageboy, "this is no serious, somber, good-literature book club. This is a raucous, almost-wet-your-pants silly, high funny group."

Many of the (GNO)2 women are prominent New Orleans mental health providers who daily probe the anguish of failed marriages, depression, and abuse. In the group, the women are

"The group has turned me on to more interesting things in this world, in this life, than anyone else. More than anyone."

relieved of their professional obligation to maintain a "blank face." Together they can be opinionated, irreverent, and outrageous.

The right mix of women took a while to evolve. They originally intended to be a group of twelve, one member to plan for each month. Now, through serendipity, they number thirteen, a baker's dozen, and have remained steady for fifteen years. No one leaves, no one enters.

(GNO)2 women have a fine appreciation of irony and wit, of low camp and high culture. From the beginning, each month's host has been responsible for one outing a year, whether a meal or some other kind of event planned in the name of fun. A swamp tour topped off by a Bloody Mary brunch. Bouts of laser tag. A whirlwind visit to New York City. An evening's lesson in poker. In honor of Rosalind's fortieth birthday, they hosted a Tupperware party where the girls' subversive humor so unnerved the poor saleswoman that she refused to return to deliver her wares, and sent someone else.

A few years back, Chris was to be married and that month (GNO)2 closed down Lulu's Beauty Salon. Feet up, champagne flowing, the girls had manicures and pedicures. Elbow to elbow, they traded tips on proper manicure technique and advised on color selection. These girls understand the zen of self-indulgence.

"The group has turned me on to more interesting things in this world, in this life, than anyone else," Marly says. "More than anyone."

For years each member would surprise the others with carefully conceived gatherings. But over time, comfortable complacency has set in. Each December, the women claim their months. They are now predictable. Brenda, whose home is on a parade route, plans a Mardi Gras party; Marianne always organizes an "escape from the summer heat" lunch and movie; and Marly and Tamara plan the December holiday celebration. Linda F., the second Linda in the group, claims January for her "day at the horse races," at which the highest winnings buy lunch.

And, of course, Linda C. claims March for the annual retreat to Thornwell. The women start looking forward to it just as soon as crayfish (usually known as "crawfish" in these parts) appear at the local markets.

The first order of business at Thornwell is always claiming beds, which seems so important, as though they will be there for an eternity. Linda arrives first and always stakes out her place on the second-floor porch. Marianne and Gail, by tradition, will join her. Out on the porch they will hear the conversations from the big bedroom all night long.

Gathered on the beds, knees drawn up under their nightgowns, the women fight all signs of exhaustion. No one wants to give up and go to sleep because they don't want to miss anything. Rosalind raises her current obsession: menopause. She asks about hot flashes. Chris says, "My husband JB was going to call emergency because my reaction was so bad." Linda F. now keeps the temperature at sixty degrees at her office; her therapy clients have all learned they must wear jackets. Robin agrees with Rosalind that temperature is not the problem; it is the enormous emotional turmoil.

The room finally goes still, as the women listen to the silence. They will wake the next morning to the great stretch of green and peacefulness lying just beyond the screen.

The women now know each other's quirks and eccentricities well. Brenda, the princess, will expect to be waited on. Her friends comply, though always with a fond remark served up in irony. There were years when Marly insisted on making lists for Thornwell, giving assignments to everyone: shopping, meals, cleanup. A sense of order. Now, after so many years, there is no need. The women just do what they want, bring what they want, cook what they want, and it all just seems to work. There is an ease to the stretch of time.

Saturday at Thornwell, a white pickup will appear midday, barreling up the driveway toward the farmhouse and lifting dust in its wake. "It must be Joe," someone will say, and everyone will jump up and race outside. Joe, Linda's cousin, raises crawfish for a living. He never fails to present (GNO)2 with a bacchanalian feast. Daddy will already be out back, bringing water to a boil in a huge stainless steel vat that has been hoisted up onto the gas burner. Two large picnic tables will be set up on the porch. Before long, big round plastic trays loaded with two hundred pounds of boiled crawfish, potatoes, and corn will be passed around.

Riffs of laughter, layers of conversation, and interrupted sentences will drift off the porch. The women will eventually summon the strength to get up from

Rosalind and Fran

the table. To stretch their legs and whet their appetite for adventure, they'll set out on a field trip to the rice dryers or to Joe's crawfish farm. And then, at the end of the day, they'll all wind up at the drive-through bar in Lake Arthur. Just like a drive-through bank. Joe has an account there and the women run up a tab. Southern women repay their debts in charm, and to repay this debt, the girls engage Joe with the latest tales from home, from the City that Care Forgot.

Thornwell provides to the (GNO)2 women a centering sense of place, derived from its rich physical beauty. They are great lovers of nature, and inevitably at some point during the weekend someone will call for a walk. The energetic ones will make their way along the rim of the rice fields, through the tangle of wild grasses, watching their feet for fear of cottonmouth snakes. Binoculars in hand, they will survey the horizon for cattle egrets and ibises alighting. Judy will usually spot some small treasure, perhaps a dried snakeskin, which she will bring home for her two girls.

Skeeter, Linda's yellow Lab, always follows behind them. One year he met a skunk while nosing around in the horse barn. Someone had to run out to the only store in town to buy big cans of tomato juice so they could bathe his coat and cut the scent. Even so, Skeeter stank all weekend and no one wanted to go near him.

Linda F. recalls her first Thornwell visit some years back. Mother of a small boy, she had had a tough time breaking free, and had planned just a single night at the farm. But once she got there, "Well, everything was so wicked good." She sank into a scalding bubble bath in the old porcelain tub perched on clawed feet in the downstairs bathroom. Her mind was made up. She called home and told her husband, "I'm sorry, Joe. But I can't come back yet. I just can't get out of this tub."

In striking counterpoint to the relaxed solace of Thornwell, every year the women also celebrate Mardi Gras together. Last year the women began the season with their own party chez Marly. Purple, green, and gold banners were strung loosely around the wooden porch railing of her home just off the parade route. Candle lanterns flickered along the brick walkway leading to the front door of the double shotgun, a traditional New Orleans style home. Inside, at the far end of the double parlor by the fireplace, a table was set with faded antique china. A rainbow shot of confetti was strewn across the tablecloth. Thirteen wine glasses were adorned with ribbons. The glasses were tagged in gold with the names of some of the Mardi Gras krewes, the social clubs that plan and march in the parades: Bacchus, Zulu, Iris, Comus, Momus, Carrollton, Rex.

For Mardi Gras, the women include their partners, children, and friends in their revelry. Several of the women's homes are situated along the parade routes. The importance of having a "home base," with bathroom, food, and parking, cannot be overlooked. Iris, an all-women krewe, always rides Saturday at noon, and Judy's office is well positioned to watch this parade. Every year she serves tea sandwiches, Zapp's spicy potato chips, "king cake" (an old Mardi Gras tradition that originated in France), and beer. She drags ladders out to the neutral ground—the St. Charles Avenue median where the trolleys run—to allow the children to climb above the crowd and catch a glimpse of the parade as it passes by. The women use the children as bait for the Mardi Gras beads that are flung into the crowds.

Last year after watching the Iris parade, the women and their families reconvened at Brenda's for Endymion, the next parade. A huge cast-iron pot of jambalaya simmered on the stove. As the parade came into view, they all rushed out of the house fighting their way to the front of the crowd, ten people deep. They all wanted to see the king, usually a movie star or rock singer. Hours later, after the floats, flambeau, and marching bands had finally passed, everyone wandered back to Brenda's. The next day were more parades and more parties: Tucks in the morning at Marly and Greg's and Bacchus that evening at Chris and JB's grand home off St. Charles Avenue.

On Mardi Gras Day itself, called Fat Tuesday, the women and their families meet early and head down St. Charles Avenue to the French Quarter, alongside the parades and masked revelers. They always dress in a group costume, conceived in wit. Rosalind, loves a pun. Last year they collectively dressed as a "gene pool": Mr. Greenjeans; Gene Kelly; Blue Jeans; Jean Harlow; a dominant and a recessive gene.

"But of course, my partner didn't want to be the recessive gene," Tamara recalls with a grin. "We bickered all the way down St. Charles Avenue. I was abandoned as soon as we arrived in the French Quarter." She laughs as she describes herself standing, whip in hand, with no one at the end of her leather leash. "It took me all day to reassert my role as dominatrix and to find my date."

Most of the (GNO)2 women are southern by birth. While proud of their roots, they admit that there is something about being a southern woman that can be limiting. "In the South it is more acceptable for women to be incompetent than impolite," observes Robin. "There are definite notions of the life you are to

"I was taught to take care of others before myself. This group has taught me to acknowledge my own needs, desires, and ambitions."

lead." Born in the conservative town of Baton Rouge, Robin's looks reflect her membership in the Junior League. "In college, I belonged to the most popular sorority. We lived in a beautiful antebellum mansion where dinner was prepared by black houseboys. As I got older, I realized I couldn't fit into that world. (GNO)2 saved me."

"Yeah," Judy adds, "but Robin still knows how to apply her makeup like a sorority sister." Robin beams a lipstick-red smile. "It is really difficult having convention and propriety so narrowly define the life you are to lead," Rosalind says. Rosalind was born in the deep South; her mother owned Maxine's, an elegant ladies' dress shop in Mobile, Alabama. Like many southern women, she was raised to become somebody's wife. (GNO)2's collection of strong women broadened her sense of possibility. "I was taught to take care of others before myself. This group has taught me to acknowledge my own needs, desires, and ambitions," she says.

Bound by a dominance of spirit, (GNO)2 women ride roughshod over the rules of what a southern woman is expected to be. "GNO taught me how to be a modern woman," Rosalind comments. "I learned that it was okay to laugh at myself and to use words that no proper southern woman would be caught dead saying. I learned from these women how to handle an argument, how to stand up for my own thoughts and ideas. This group has opened up my life." Rosalind has recently completed her PhD and is teaching women's history at Tulane University.

Always, just beyond the frivolity that so characterizes them, lies a depth of feeling, a soulfulness born of experience. "In many ways, GNO reflects the larger world with all of its problems and paradoxes," Rosalind observes. Within this group there are second and third marriages. Battles with infertility, many lost, one won. The loss of brothers, sisters, and parents. Changes in sexual orientation (twice as many dates on a Saturday night), and then, changes back again. These women embrace life lived large, undeterred by the risks. "We have hit milestones together," Rosalind reflects. This year the women turned forty, fifty,

Marly, Brenda, and Rosalind

and sixty. "As a group," she continues, "we are witnessing what it is like to hit those milestones, and we are role models for one another in celebrating them."

While celebration is paramount, the decadent tendencies of (GNO)2 do not always accommodate the individual needs of its women. Some members perceive a carelessness toward the struggles felt when maternal roles collide with (GNO)2 frivolity. "I love these women," says Linda F., "but some of them don't comprehend the demands of being a parent. I'm torn myself by my loss of freedom, but sometimes I feel unsupported by this group."

The issue of children has been a source of significant pain for many of these women. Several struggled for years to overcome infertility. Of a baker's dozen, only two group members have children. No one dares ask anymore whether children are welcome at (GNO)2 outings, except those traditionally open to families. The women are strongly divided over the issue, and the debate just became too intense. They are aware that in the years ahead, if the group is to hold together, they will need to adapt as the life circumstances of members change.

Yet the (GNO)2 women do not back away from examining their own choices in life. This past February, the group met for the first time at one woman's new apartment. She had just left her lover of seven years, having left one husband for that relationship, and having left another husband years before. At this simple Saturday lunch, the women confronted the hardest truth. Regret. Of long ago leaving a first husband. Of never having children. Of not having ever married. Of errant life choices that can never be undone.

"I can't let myself have regrets," one woman says brightly. "If I did, I would just kill myself." The women laugh at the joke, then shift a bit.

You have to listen carefully to these women. Turn your head and you may miss a revelation, a secret never before told, and perhaps never to be told again. At a recent gathering, one woman spoke of the challenges of being a stepmother, and of the seriousness of her stepson's problems—his abusive behavior and crossing of lines. She spoke of her husband's pain, of how he numbed himself with alcohol. For years she had told no one. That day she told the women she didn't know if she would stay.

In true (GNO)2 fashion, the intensity of that moment was broken by raucous conversation. Linda recounted how her mother, Eloise, had cut up all of her brassieres and the elastic on her pants. She was, Linda explained, just so tired of feeling uncomfortable and constrained that she grabbed a pair of scissors and started cutting. The women rowdily cheered this liberating feat. Eloise passed away just last year.

Ask any member and you will hear that (GNO)2 is a source of great strength and healing. When Gail had lost her father, and then her mother got so sick, she couldn't speak with anyone, she just couldn't. But there was a message on her phone machine from every GNOer. When Linda was stricken with cancer, non-Hodgkin's lymphoma, it scared all of them. "There were two full months of tests," Linda recalls, "and all of the girls were so individually supportive, calling me, making sure I was all right. Before the surgery, the GNO girls took me out for lunch and gave me little gifts to show their love and to brighten my spirits. It was like the pregame huddle. There was this amazing energy coming from all of these women. It lifted me up and made me realize I was ready to face the game."

The degree of connection among these women is palpable. The meaning of this group has changed over and over again through the years. Marly says, "At first I was thrilled just to make new friends. I don't think any of us realized how emotionally involved we might become. These women satisfy my need for a certain intensity and closeness, a need that even my own husband cannot fully meet. Every woman in GNO is someone I respect. Each is strong and good and admirable in her own right. I wear my place in this group like a badge of honor."

These strong sentiments are shared throughout the group. At the final meal at Thornwell, Brenda rises to her feet and remarks on the rich, complicated texture of the group bond. "GNO women are forever getting their act together," she observes. "Sometimes raw, sometimes reticent, GNO women are always real."

Brenda tearily confides that there have been times when she has wanted to quit the group because, with such intense connectedness, there is often also pain. "But the important piece is that I'm still here," Brenda says. "I go to GNO as if to a feast."

As another Thornwell weekend draws to a close, the women engage in one final ritual: stripping the beds and washing the linens for next year's visit. No one will sleep in these beds until they return.

The women each fold laundry differently. Burying their hands in the warm comfort of linens pulled straight from the dryer, they compare notes. Some proceed carefully, methodically, folding and smoothing until the sheets resemble neat rectangles. Others flap the sheets wildly in front of them and then hook them under their chins, folding quickly hand over hand. The conversation turns to their mothers, their grandmothers, and their childhood homes, where such habits were first acquired. For these women, even matters as simple as these have a certain resonance, an importance in life.

(GNO)2. Greater New Orleans Girls' Night Out. Only in the South would they be called girls. Because they are clearly Southern women.

front row, from left: Theoria ("Lady T"), Frances ("Smiley"), Frances ("Frankie"); *back row, from left:* Pearl ("Ms. Pearl"), Andrea ("A.J."), Frances ("Franlee"); Julia ("Cookie"), Deniece ("Nee Nee"), Ellen ("Sunshine")

The Phenomenal Ladies Motorcycle Club

PRINCE GEORGES COUNTY, MARYLAND

I am always afraid," admits one of the Phenomenal Ladies, "but it gets you to the other side of freedom."

Staring down your fears and riding right through them. Laying miles of blacktop between you and the hassles of life. The agency to take any turn you please or travel straight ahead. The sense of endless possibility. The exhilarating physicality of speed. The sting of the wind in your face, the roar and the heat and vibration of the engine beneath you. And the comfort, the ease, of doing it with other women. Women who appreciate your fears—and your desire for freedom. It is the freedom to ride, daring to do what you love in life.

Meeting the ten Phenomenal Ladies, you are struck by how their lives mirror those of most American women. They are conventional and responsible. Ranging in age from thirty-five to sixty, many have been married, some divorced, one widowed. Most have raised their children and now speak proudly of their grandchildren. Pearl has great-grandchildren. In this group you find a retired science teacher and a manager, two postal supervisors, a mail carrier, a medical supply warehouse foreman, an accountant, and a day-care teacher. They attend church on Sunday. Many sing with the choir. Pearl sings in two.

You would expect this group of women to bowl together, to sew together, to shop together, which of course they do. What you would not expect is for them to ride together. On their own motorcycles. And not in the back but always, always in the front.

If you ask them about their bikes, their alter egos emerge and the mischief starts to dance in their eyes. They begin to tease and strut and to boast about their motorcycles. "Smiley's got the newest bike, and the best one," explains Ellen, nicknamed Sunshine. Sunshine talks low, under her breath, and walks solidly in her black leather boots, with an air of confidence. "A brand-new Harley. She's got a bike that a lot of men would love to own."

Smiley flashes a blinding smile. "Of course, I'd let any of these ladies ride it if they want to. They are all my sisters." Smiley proudly describes the twelve-by-twelve-foot wooden shed her husband built in their backyard to house her Harley. "It's called the Hog House."

The Phenomenal Ladies Motorcycle Club of Prince Georges County, Maryland, was founded in 1998. But most of the members have biked together for nearly a decade. "Our ladies like to ride long distances," says Lady T. "It's challenging. It requires a big commitment. We'll travel several states to visit and support other women's motorcycle clubs."

Lady T, her black and gray curls arranged carefully around her shoulders, is the president of the Phenomenal Ladies. She is voted in as their leader year after year. At first blush, Lady T appears quiet, but she is not shy. Her poised, dignified demeanor keeps everyone in line.

There is little pressure in this group and few rules. Each lady must own a bike. Lady T and Franlee each own two. There are five Harleys, four Hondas, two Yamahas, and one Suzuki. The women must attend one club function a month—a fund-raiser or, best of all, a ride. There are six officers, elected every two years.

During their first meeting, held within a week of their decision to form the group, the women thought carefully about their identity. They didn't want to be like a lot of other clubs. In this group there would be no smoking, no cussing, no daredevil stunts. A road captain would ensure that on their road trips, they would ride in proper formation. They are very careful on the road, always looking out for one another and making sure that they stay together as a group.

"We knew we had to choose the right name, something that would fit us," Lady T explains. "Everyone wrote down different names. Then finally Wanda opened the dictionary, and found the word *phenomenal*. The definition was 'outstanding.' That was it, we all agreed, and we've been phenomenal ever since."

The group proudly wears custom-designed black leather vests when they ride. "When you ride the distance, you need protection from the wind," Lady T explains. "So, when we became Phenomenal Ladies we had to design our new motorcycle vests. And, of course, choose our colors. Frankie said that if we are phenomenal, we need a crown." The women all turn around to show off their black leather vests. There on the back, decorated in brilliant colors of turquoise and fuchsia, is the striking face of an African queen wearing a crown and riding her motorcycle.

Watching the Phenomenal Ladies assemble for a ride, you witness a remarkable transformation, a visible process of empowerment. Donning black leather and fringe, balancing six hundred pounds of motorcycle on the heels of their boots, revving their engines with the slightest turn of their wrists, these lovely, respectable women become biker chicks. Riding together allows the Phenomenal Ladies to push at the edges of their own identities, to play with who they are. They reveal their inner souls, uninhibited. They acquire a sense of power that remains with them, in a quieter way, even after they've taken off their vests, parked their bikes, and reentered their everyday lives.

Riding in formation, dressed identically in their club vests and colors, the

Phenomenal Ladies are a dazzling sight to behold. And they are obviously proud of their image.

"We ride with class and style," Smiley states with assurance. "We get a lot of attention in our vests and colors. We cruise through towns slowly and wave. Women always smile and give us thumbs-up as we pass." With their high visibility, the Phenomenal Ladies serve as role models for other women, encouraging them to take steps toward independence they might not otherwise take. "Yeah," says Lady T. "You see women pointing at us and saying, 'Look, it's a woman biker. Isn't that wonderful?' And I always answer back, 'Yes, it is wonderful. So what's stopping you?'"

"You see women pointing at us and saying, 'Look, it's a woman biker. Isn't that wonderful?' And I always answer back, 'Yes, it is wonderful. So what's stopping you?'"

The Phenomenal Ladies have struggled hard for respect and recognition. Not only do they inspire other women but they support and inspire one another. Pearl recalls that she rode for many years with two "men's clubs." Even though the clubs were coed, the men never acknowledged that fact, and they weren't encouraging to her. "I rode with them, but it's as if I didn't exist. I felt invisible," she recalls.

"Yeah, the guys who see us always assume that our bikes belong to our men, and we're just polishing them," says Candy. She points a manicured fingernail to a button pinned to her vest. It announces in bold black letters: THIS IS NOT MY BOYFRIEND'S MOTORCYCLE.

The women each came to riding motorcycles at different points in their lives and for different reasons. Some learned from friends, some from their men, and others were just pulled to the sense of freedom. Lady T recalls how, in the mid-

Frankie and Lady T

1970s, her then husband came home with a brand-new motorcycle—and one helmet. "I marched right out to Kmart and bought my own helmet." Lady T took her first ride on the back of her husband's motorcycle. "I closed my eyes the whole time," she recalls with humor. "Well, I got tired of riding on the back," she continues, "so I bought myself a bike, even before I knew how to turn on the ignition. I signed up for lessons, and I've been riding ever since. For me, riding means independence."

"When I first started, women weren't riding," remarks Sunshine. She got her motorcycle license more than thirty-five years ago, having watched a guy in the neighborhood ride and thinking how much fun it would be. She bought a 350 Honda, then a 500 Honda, and now owns a Suzuki Intruder with an 800-cubic centimeter engine.

Another member learned to ride over a decade ago. "I was going with this guy. He would take me to this little bar called the Bottom." Since the 1950s, the Bottom, in Racing Springs, Maryland, has been the place where area bikers congregate. "He used to leave me on the back of the bike. I'd say to him, 'Why can't I go in with you?' 'Because you don't have your own bike,' he'd say. So I said to myself right then and there, 'How do I learn?' I was a backseat rider, but I decided to be a front seat driver."

Though most came to motorcycles through men, the Phenomenal Ladies found riding a means of independence from them. Candy, the retired science teacher, took her first ride on the back of her boyfriend's bike in 1970. "We stayed together for twenty years. But he was looking for a wife, so we agreed to disagree. I bought a bike, he got a wife, and we're all good friends."

"Men want you to ride when and where they ride, and then they want you to stay at home," Candy adds. "But we're never at home. We're on our bikes riding with one another."

"Yes," Lady T observes, "we spend most of our free time together. I used to have a garden before I started to ride. I don't have time for that anymore." The Phenomenal Ladies share a desire to expand the boundaries of what has been presented to them in life. Together they have made their world much bigger.

Riding together, even a short distance, transports the Phenomenal Ladies far from the everyday. "If I'm feeling restless or unhappy, I can call up these women," explains Lady T. "All we have to do is ride a few miles down the highway to the park. We can just lay a sheet on the ground, hang out there for half an hour, and my world is changed." Pearl, at age sixty, adds, "I work at a hospice and I see a lot of people die. Riding with these women is such a release. I can leave my worries behind."

The Phenomenal Ladies do not need to ride far to find freedom. But they do ride the distance. These women are seeing the world together. Each year they log thousands of miles on cross-country road trips. They have ridden their bikes from the Washington, D.C., area to Greenville, South Carolina; Asheville, North Carolina; and Atlanta, Georgia. They pulled their bikes by trailer to Daytona Beach, Florida, and Stafford, Texas.

Their toughest ride was coming home from Louisville, Kentucky. Thirteen hours in the driving rain. "A.J. had never ridden in the rain before," says Frankie. "I was riding behind her and I noticed that her rain pants were smoking. They were pressed up against her hot exhaust pipe. So we hollered for her to stop and taped them up for the rest of the ride." The women hope their next ride will be easier, especially for A.J.

Mobility brings freedom and empowerment, but not without challenge. The elements are tough and the long rides require physical endurance, which the women must dig deep within themselves to find. Aching joints and arthritis intrude on many a ride. Candy admits that she is often tempted to give up the road. But the other women prod her on.

And then there is fear. "I have a few phobias, especially when it comes to

our long-distance rides," admits Lady T. "But they don't stop us from riding. We help each other through." One of the ladies is afraid of tunnels. "The whole way through, I just scream and cry into my helmet." The other women ride in formation to surround and support her.

Lady T fears mountains and bridges. "On one trip we had to cross the Chesapeake Bay Bridge. So, without any fuss, Sunshine rode my bike across the bridge. She hitched a ride back, and then rode her own bike across to join us." Lady T smiles at her friend, all fondness and appreciation. "Another time when we were coming home from Huntsville, Alabama, I rode down a big mountain on Route Forty. I had the mountain in front of me and a tractor-trailer behind me. I was so scared, I rode my brakes the whole way down. When we finally stopped, I just went into the bathroom and cried and cried. But then I got back on my bike and went the distance. With my sisters."

Mindful of the risks of the road, the Phenomenal Ladies participate each spring in the blessing of the bikes. Huge crowds of bikers gather in a local park. The deafening roar of engines is silenced as the minister—himself a biker— prays quietly for their safety and well-being throughout the year. The Phenomenal Ladies always take up a collection for the families of those who have been injured.

The bonds of riding together have spilled over into other parts of their lives. The women have become one another's best friends. They talk on the phone. They go out together. "And we don't go anywhere without stopping to shop," says Lady T. "We never go on any road trip without our luggage and bungee cords for our purchases."

"We make the money we want and we can spend it on what we want," Pearl continues. "And if we're not together, we shop for each other. We like to dress alike. We know each other's taste. If you buy one, you buy ten." "Yeah," Frankie complains, "we are always writing checks to each other. When you leave a club meeting, your arms are always filled with new things and you are always broke."

The Phenomenal Ladies do not simply spend their time and money on themselves, however. They often ride the distance for a good cause. Each year they attend, among other fund-raising rallies, the Mid-Atlantic Women's Motorcycle Rally, which attracts hundreds of women bikers to raise money for breast cancer research. "The motorcycle circle sticks together. If someone in any club needs help, the others are there," says Pearl. "We love supporting other women bikers. There is so much camaraderie. It's like we are all sisters."

The Phenomenal Ladies raise money for their own favorite causes, chosen by club vote, by hosting an annual Trophy Party. Held at the volunteer fire department, this big dance party kicks off at 10:00 P.M. with a DJ, raffles, and prizes and runs to the wee hours of the morning. First prizes are awarded to those who have traveled the farthest distance "on two wheels," and to the clubs who are most represented, both in and out of state. A donation is required. This year the proceeds will benefit children's health.

The Phenomenal Ladies consider themselves a hand-picked family. "I'm like a big sister to some of the ladies, and a little sister to others," observes Lady T.

"I love these women. We understand each other. Men are the cause of so much pain. The Phenomenal Ladies are my friends for life."

"We do get mad at each other," she concedes, "because everyone's got their own ways. At least eighty percent of the club is either going through the change or has PMS. But if we do have a disagreement, we keep going. We don't hold a grudge. If the ladies bicker, we simply ask, 'Are you phenomenal or not?'"

And, of course, in times of challenge the Phenomenal Ladies are a source of unerring support. When Frankie was diagnosed with leukemia she hit a wall, physically and emotionally. Out of work for seven months, she struggled through chemotherapy and suffered the indignity of losing all of her hair. "These women were so great, visiting me in the hospital, bringing sunshine into my day," she recalls. Frankie was released from the hospital in January and she thought she'd never get on her bike again. But in June, the women came around to her house and took her on a ride. "We went all the way to Charlottesville, Virginia. I was so exhausted when I got home that I slept for three days straight. But I am so thankful that these ladies pushed me. Because they gave me back my confidence and my freedom," she says warmly.

Life changes quickly, and it can take you by surprise. Sunshine, at age fifty-five, never expected to be raising children a second time. Yet just when she thought she could do as she pleased, ride as she liked, she found herself raising her son's children. Joshua is seven; Isaiah is ten. Their mother died and now Sunshine has custody. This new responsibility has largely taken her off the road, but it has only brought the Phenomenal Ladies deeper into her life. Lady T teaches the kids how to help their grandmother. Last week it was folding laundry. "Next week I'm going to teach them how to iron, so that Sunshine can sit down sometimes," she says.

The Phenomenal Ladies Motorcycle Club has become a lifeline, an anchor for each of its members. "I love these women," Pearl remarks quietly. "We understand each other. Men are the cause of so much pain. The Phenomenal Ladies are my friends for life. I feel that this won't ever end."

"A good friend of mine died recently," says Lady T. "It made it all so clear. I am going to die too sometime. I might as well be doing what I like with people I love. I am going to ride with these women for as long as I can throw my leg over my bike."

Today, the brilliant sun and the warm breeze conspire with the Phenomenal Ladies for their next adventure. Pulling on her motorcycle helmet as they gear up for a ride, Lady T laments the only downside to riding the distance with her friends. With a playful smile she points to the bar pin attached to her vest. It reads: HAIRDO BY HELMET.

The Mother-Daughter Book Group

SEATTLE, WASHINGTON

Mika opens the conversation by taking hold of the talking stick. It is a gourd her father brought back from Zimbabwe. The girls think of it as a "wand of wisdom," and pass it around to give each other the floor—oh, yes, and their mothers, too. Mika asks, "Would you like Robin as a friend, why and why not?"

This evening will center around a discussion of friendship, among friends and across generations. The group is meeting in Mika and her mother's home, and therefore, as is the tradition of this mother-daughter book group, the book they are discussing was selected by Mika and her mother, Ruthann. Tonight's book is *Ribbons*, by Laurence Yep. It tells the story of a young girl who loves ballet but must give up her dance lessons in order to help her family bring her grandmother to the United States.

"I think I would like Robin. She was kind and generous as a friend." Mika answers her own question. "Robin gave her ballet ribbons to her girlfriend so that she could dance in her toe shoes." She passes the gourd to her friend Suzanna. "I would and wouldn't want to be her friend," says Suzanna. "I wouldn't because she seems too obsessed with ballet, but then again she seems like a good friend." Ruthann adds, "Robin has good core qualities."

Julia's mother, Jeanne, an elementary-school teacher who has a wonderful way of asking the girls thought-provoking questions, takes the floor. "I am most

nt row, from left: Karin, Suzanna, Mika, Ruthann; *back row, from left:* Abby, Melissa, Sara, Carol

drawn to people who have passion, whether they are my passions or not, because they cause me to grow. And Robin's loyalty impressed me."

The conversation flows freely between the generations in this group, the mothers and daughters speaking up and interjecting their thoughts without hesitation.

This mother-daughter book group was formed two years ago, when the girls were all in fifth grade at the same elementary school, on Mercer Island off the coast of Seattle. The mothers were looking ahead to the tender and difficult middle-school years. They wanted to make sure that their daughters had a sense of connection and would develop a strong sense of self. As Emily's mother, Marny, observes, "The books are the hinge, but there are really other motivations." Abby's mother, Karin, who first spoke with Ruthann about founding the group, adds, "We said, 'Let's get this going—before our daughters wander away from us.'"

"The girls hear us talking about issues that they don't usually hear us discuss, like relationships and life challenges. They see us having substantive conversations among women, not just going shopping together."

"We all hope to be role models for the girls," says Karin. The mothers are providing for their daughters the example of strong female relationships and the valuing of these relationships. As Karin explains, "The girls hear us talking about issues that they don't usually hear us discuss, like relationships and life challenges. They see us having substantive conversations among women, not just going shopping together."

The mothers have discovered yet another important opportunity. They can impart wisdom to their daughters without appearing to lecture them. As

Suzanna's mother, Carol, says, "We can tell our stories into the atmosphere so that they don't land on our own daughters, so that they don't have to react."

The teen years are, as the mothers recognize, often self-conscious and filled with emotion. Each hopes that her daughter will feel that through the group she has many resources; that if she is wary of approaching her own mother to discuss an unsettling issue or a personal concern, the others would be available for her to seek out. Marny recalls, "I remember one daughter confiding to me that she had been having a really hard time sleeping. I talked to her about what was bothering her. And ultimately I was able to ask, 'Have you talked to your own mom about it?'"

"My daughter is not very conversational. She doesn't talk easily with me about ideas and feelings," another mother reveals. She joined the group to do something substantive with her daughter, to offer an outlet for her daughter to open up. The mothers have come to understand and respect each other's parenting styles, and they have learned how to complement one another and provide helpful differences in perspective and approach.

The mothers represent a remarkable array of role models for the girls. Among them are women who have each set out to obtain very different but important goals in life and have brought them to fruition, from being good mothers and civic and community leaders to becoming successful professionals, including a judge, a teacher, a lawyer, and a social worker. A few of the mothers have faced significant physical challenges and continue undeterred.

The group decided early on to read books about strong girls and strong women. The book selection is made by the younger hostess of the month, and that daughter is also responsible for developing a list of questions and guiding the discussion. Some of the members are avid readers, while others are not, and many are introduced to books they would never have discovered on their own. Though the evenings usually begin with the girls and moms hanging out and catching up with one another in separate groups, once they come together for the discussion, everyone becomes absorbed. To structure their conversations, they use the talking stick. No one can interrupt the person holding the stick. "It's a temporary moment of power," Marny explains. "That's very important for these girls, who are at an age when they are just finding their voice."

Tonight, everyone is convened in Ruthann and Mika's living room. A huge wall of floor-to-ceiling windows look out on tall pine trees. The room is filled with artifacts reflecting the blending of Japanese and Jewish cultures in their heritage and in their home. Mika passes a plate of pink sticky-rice treats. "It's called mochi," she volunteers. They are a Japanese tradition at New Year's.

Mika is well prepared for their discussion. Her questions are all neatly typed out, as well as her own answers. The book she selected, *Ribbons*, has some special resonance for her and her mother. Mika explains that she identifies somewhat with the main character, because they are both of mixed race. "I am of Japanese and Jewish heritage. I also know what it's like having an obligation to my elders, especially my grandparents. But, I don't identify in other ways. I am more privileged than Robin is in the book. If I wanted to go to summer sports camp, my parents would send me."

When her mother, Ruthann, gets the gourd, she adds, "I am a third-generation Japanese American woman." Ruthann's grandmother immigrated to the United States from Japan at the turn of the century to obtain better schooling. Ruthann's mother was very involved with civil rights and peace and social justice, and Ruthann herself is a leader in the Japanese-Jewish community. "In Asian culture, sons and boys come first. I still feel a certain obligation to my parents that I think my brothers don't have. I still do all of the work for the family at holidays and for family events. Mika questions this. And the truth is, I got mixed messages about how independent I could be, because my mother was an amazing role model and so was my grandmother."

Julia and her mom, Jeanne

While every teenage girl is involved in the hard work of defining her own identity, many of these girls must also grapple with questions of cultural identity, as most come from multicultural homes. Marny reflects on conversations that many of the books have stimulated. "We cross religions and cultures within our homes. We talk about the frustrations and joys related to holidays and celebration within our own families. The issues of inclusion and exclusion." Ruthann adds, "Mika and I, we talk about cultures and relationships a lot; it is good for Mika to hear other perspectives from her friends."

There are many differences between the pairs of mothers and daughters in the group. Some want the conversation to be focused and intellectual; others are more comfortable talking about feelings. In deference to all, they talk about both.

Much of the discussion tonight concerns issues of privilege and deprivation.

"The books and the discussion force thoughts from the girls and the moms that we wouldn't ordinarily have together, at a critical time in the girls' lives. I am so impressed with the depth of thoughts and feelings we share."

The mothers have varying degrees of comfort about the sheltered, fortunate lives they have offered their daughters on Mercer Island. Marny's daughter, Emily, comments, "I have had to give up a lot since my grandma died because my mom now does a lot for my grandfather, cooking for him and taking care of him. She is not at home as much." But as the group discusses, such sacrifices are relatively minor compared to some of those faced by the girls they read about. The mothers guide their daughters to read books about girls who have had to live in broken homes or whose families are poor. "The books help us talk about struggles and envy," Carol explains. "What does money mean in terms of happiness? They allow the girls to see different worlds."

"Our book group has become a safe place to talk," Marny observes. "We have a lot of common values and mutual respect. We have all learned to listen carefully to each other."

Listening carefully, the girls talk about fear. Marny gets them started by admitting that she could relate to Robin's character in the book. "I remember so many situations when I was young, when I wouldn't speak up and ask for help. I had all sorts of resentments and fears." Marny prompts the girls, "Do you remember being scared or angry and not talking to your parents?" The girls each in turn express their fears, from robbers under the bed, to going to the doctor, a fire in the middle of the night, and a screaming bus driver. Mika says, "I remember when I was learning to read, I was scared of the big huge letters. Then I had a nightmare about it. I thought I was sick. I was afraid the letters would come after me." Marny asks, "Your dream, was that a turning point?" "Yes," Mika responds.

One girl quietly confides, "I used to be scared of being held back a grade at school. I'm still scared when I get my report card. I am afraid of teachers, kind of. When I get to know people, I can be really outgoing, but when I am at school, I'm like a turtle hiding in my shell. I don't come out." The girls giggle together at the image of the turtle friend in her shell. Then Jeanne pulls the conversation back to the book. "When there is conflict with individuals, I have a hard time standing up for myself, or even my opinions, like Robin." The other mothers nod. "At least you girls have learned to respectfully say if you don't like your friend's book selection. That's a good start," Marny adds.

Reading books together has also provided the girls with opportunities to glimpse into their mothers' hearts. As Julia, Jeanne's daughter, recalls, "I read one book out loud with my mom and all of a sudden my mom would start to cry." Jeanne responds, "When I would get emotional, Julia would stop and ask me why."

Suzanna, Mika, Abby, and Melissa

As Marny notes, "The books and the discussion force thoughts from all of us—the girls and the moms—that we wouldn't ordinarily have together, at a critical time in the girls' lives. I am so impressed with the depth of thoughts and feelings we share."

Along the way, the mothers and daughters have found many commonalities in their lives. About half of the girls in the group are adopted. This came out one evening during a book discussion. "And the book wasn't even about adoption," recalls Jeanne. Mika was asking the questions that evening, too, and one of her questions was, "If you could write a letter to anyone, who would it be?" Three of the girls immediately said they would write to their birth mothers. Terri, Tammy's mother, responded, "I would write your birth mother too, and tell her how neat you are."

That night the girls launched into a discussion of how they imagine their birth mothers. "The books bring up a lot of issues, but they are once removed and that makes it a little safer," Jeanne comments. "It's not quite like looking at yourself in the mirror."

During most evenings the girls eventually run off to play basketball or some other game among themselves, and the mothers turn to their own conversation. They talk about local politics, school issues, work, and their kids. Sometimes they share observations about their girls and help each other out with parenting strategies. Often one of the other mothers can see something in one of the girls that her own mother has missed. As Sara, Melissa's mother, notes, "Our conversations help me be a better parent."

On some evenings, the mothers are inspired to reflect on their own childhoods. They will discuss the impact their childhood experiences have had on them as adults and in turn how those experiences may be passed down to their daughters. "Part of this group," Jeanne says thoughtfully, "is us processing our own childhoods and then thinking about our daughters. We often remember our own struggles to fit in. The girls are now at an age when fitting in is so important."

This group of mothers and daughters has created a special sphere of intimacy and mutual respect that bridges the generational divide. "It's all so impressionistic," Carol reflects. "I remember so many moments, the looks on the girls' faces. Or the tears in a mom's eyes when a story is being told." As Marny concludes, "The evening always begins with the girls huddled together on one side of the room. But as the night progresses, they rearrange themselves. Our daughters come closer to us. We all cozy up at the end."

left to right (adults): Megan, Lisa, Ellie, Andrea, Beth, Melanie

The Fabulous Group

If you want something in your life, you have to be able to envision it." Ellie describes one of the most powerful rituals her women's group has created in its twelve years together, a ritual that has changed her life.

"It wasn't just wishing, it was more intentional," Ellie continues. "First we meditated. We sat quietly to clear our minds and open ourselves to thoughts of how we would like life to be. We each went off on our own for half an hour. We wrote down our dreams in the active voice, as though they were really happening. Then we came together and read them out loud."

That was the second overnight for the Fabulous Group. The women rented a house on Bodega Bay, north of San Francisco. The house was on a quiet, dead-end lane, close enough to the Pacific Ocean that they could hear the forceful pounding of the waves and taste the salt in the air. Huge windows overlooked cliffs, ocean, and parkland.

"There is power in saying it out loud. Articulating your dreams allows you to make movement toward them," Beth notes. "When barriers come up," Lisa adds, "those who witnessed your wishes are able to support you, to encourage you."

The women extended the ritual by making "power sticks," which symbolized their dreams. They decorated them with colorful ribbons, then stood at the edge of the cliff and tossed the sticks into the ocean.

The women call this ritual "manifesting." It's about creating a sense of possibility. You say it out loud; you do it; and it becomes real. A testament to the ritual's power is the fact that all of the things the women wished for that day have come to pass. "Ginie, who moved away from us, imagined herself in Maine, in a room with a huge loom. And I remember saying that I wanted to be part of a community, to own a home," says Lisa. "My husband and I thought we could never own our own place. But now we do." Ellie imagined a baby in a backpack. Now she is a single mom at forty-three. She named her daughter Reilly, after her grandmother. "Having a group like this, voicing my dreams in front of these women, allowed Reilly to come true. I don't want to overstate things," Ellie continues, "but I never would have had a child on my own. These women gave me courage. They allowed me to take the leap of faith."

"I don't want to overstate things, but I never would have had a child on my own. These women gave me courage. They allowed me to take the leap of faith."

Reflective of the culture of their home in the Bay Area of northern California, these women are socially conscious and earthy. Mostly teachers and journalists, they were drawn together by a desire to honor something bigger than themselves, outside the confines of institutionalized religion. Andrea and Laura were good friends, and they began talking about wanting a formal way of bringing spirituality into their lives. Ellie, who was new in town, met Ginie skiing, and in time they also started talking about their desire for more spirituality. Recognizing their common interests, Laura decided to hold a meeting at her home in Oakland. When she wrote down the list of women to invite, she penned "The Fabulous Group" at the top of the page. Though tongue-in-cheek, the name somehow stuck. The women soon found a regular venue in Andrea's art studio, a large industrial space with wide windows.

Their early years together were consumed with creating ritual. All of the women were single and in their twenties. Andrea remembers, "We were young and restless and we all had a good deal of energy and time." They met every week for at least three years, on Tuesdays, at the same space. They feel the secret to their longevity as a group is the intensity of this time spent together. In those days, the women tried anything that came to mind for group activities. They gave each other license to experiment. "We tried different art projects, making masks and goddess sculptures, working with pastels and clay," Andrea notes. "Periodically we would meet on a Saturday and bring in guests to conduct workshops on topics like yoga or dreamwork. But most of all, we centered on ritual." They drew on many different approaches to the spiritual: Buddhism, chakras, relaxation exercises, movement and dance. "Every time was a big discovery," Megan says, "trying new things."

"It was wild and exciting and a little bit scary. We danced and we howled and we beat on drums," Ellie recalls. "It was a wild bacchanal."

Laura was a powerful force in the group's early years. "She has such presence," Lisa says. "Laura is over six feet tall, and she brought this incredible energy." Laura introduced traditions from ancient religions she had read about that draw inspiration from the elements of the earth and the cycles of nature. "There was a sense of the illicit about it," admits Ellie, "a feeling of the seriousness of it. These traditions are so misunderstood in popular culture." "We feared the stereotypes and were a bit freaked out about it," Lisa remembers, "but it all seemed very potent."

Planned activities created a certain amount of performance anxiety, but at the same time, the activities allowed those who weren't as close to get to know one another more quickly. "We planned in pairs, with different women each time," says Melanie.

Laura introduced one of the rituals that has endured throughout the years. Each time the group meets, they begin with what they refer to as a grounding ritual, "calling in the directions." "We never 'call the directions' the same way twice," Andrea describes. "We have a set of agreed-upon ideas about what each direction—east, south, north, west—stands for. Aspects of life and human experience that we want to recognize, deepen, call into our awareness."

East represents air, the mental realm, new beginnings, clear thinking. South is fire, representing emotion, passion, creativity, and courage. West is water, the intuitive realm, which ebbs and flows, representing flexibility and access to the subconscious. And north represents earth, the physical realm. Stability, roots, connection to community, and patience.

Meeting at Megan's new house, just blocks from the Bay Bridge, the group demonstrates the ritual. The room is sparsely furnished. A huge hammered-copper gong adorns the wall above the fireplace and the warmth of lighted candles emanates from the mantel. The women first sit in a circle on the floor on large cushions, then they stand, all barefoot. They grasp each other's hands, and "ground" for their evening together. In silence, they roll onto their toes, then solidly onto the balls of their feet, trying to feel the earth beneath them, the soil and rock below. Then they "call in the directions."

Spirits of the East
Creatures of air
Bring us your powers of clarity, vision, and light
Help us to be open to new beginnings
Give us the keen vision of the hawk and the eagle
Help us to transcend the everyday and give us new perspective on our lives
Help us to soar
Join us

Spirits of the South
Creatures of fire

Bring us energy, passion, and courage
Help us to draw on these strengths and to use them wisely
Help us to feel deeply alive and connected to our inner core
Bring us your heat allowing us to burn brightly in the world
Join us

Spirits of the West
Creatures of water
Bring us your powers of deep knowing, flexibility, and change
Help us to follow our intuition always and to flow freely with the
   changing tides
Help us to find inspiration in our dreams
Guide us to our unconscious like the whale finds peace in the depths of
   the ocean
Join us

Spirits of the North
Creatures of earth
Bring us groundedness, solidity, and strength
Help us to find our roots, no matter where we are
Connect us to ourselves and to each other
Help us to reach down into the darkness, drawing power and sense of
   purpose for the greater good of all
Join us

The poetic images and rhythm induce a meditative state, a sense of calm.
"For me," reflects Andrea, "calling in the directions is about achieving a deeper
level of connection and place." "Yes," adds Beth, "some sort of universal force."
Although the women have settled on a standard invocation, the way they recite
it varies. Sometimes the women are finished quickly, other times they repeat the

phrases for several minutes. Years ago they used to call the directions by singing, but that was when they were still working out how they wanted to perform the ritual.

Not all of the women embrace each ritual they try with the same level of enthusiasm. Laura, who introduced the directions, now feels the ritual has become a bit forced. But she still participates, and that reflects the openness of spirit in this group. As committed as they are to their explorations, the women can be skeptical of some of the teachings and beliefs they encounter. "We always invoke the goddess of laughter," remarks Lisa, expressing a hint of irony the group maintains. "We are all spiritual, but there is also an intellectual edge. We are always questioning things, never buying into them all the way but finding a way to appreciate what works for us."

As the evening progresses, the women engage in another of their favorite rituals, the reading of the rune stones, an ancient Celtic tradition. The softly rounded stones have markings, each with a significance explained in *The Book of Runes*. According to the tradition, the women ask questions of the runes relating to their lives, and select three stones. They then read the related passages out loud, with a bit of interpretation.

"What do I need to do to prepare for my desire to have a child?" Andrea asks. She carefully selects and places her stones in front of her. Ellie leans over, looks at the stones, and laughs. "It's fertility; the center stone symbolizes fertility." Beth asks about the choices ahead of her. "There are so many things I want to do in my life right now, finish my dissertation, get pregnant, spend more time with my grandmother, who is ill." When she sees that she has selected the blank rune, "the unknowable," which portends death, tears come to her eyes. She asks Megan to read for her. The other stones she has selected are more hopeful, one of partnership, another of openings: "'Take heart, the process of self-change is progressing, you will gain a new sense of clarity.'" "I am so caught up," Beth

Andrea, Lisa, and Megan

reveals, "in trying to control, to anticipate, perhaps the message here is that I need to just be open to receive."

As the women got to know one another better through their initial rituals, they found themselves sharing more and more of their personal struggles. They would be discussing something and suddenly someone would be in tears. Eventually they initiated the ritual they call check-in, which has become central to their gatherings. They realize that the telling of life stories is an age-old ritual among women, and so, at every meeting, they go around in a circle and tell the story of what is happening in their lives.

As the women drew even closer, they began to extend the group ritual into their family lives. Lisa's wedding was a turning point. "I asked the women's group to give me away," Lisa recalls. "My father hadn't been very supportive, so when my husband and I decided to get married, I asked these women to walk down the aisle with me instead. I felt very vulnerable, divulging how important they were to my life." "We were all so psyched," Ellie interrupts. "We all wore white." Before they entered the chapel, the women gathered around Lisa and performed a grounding. Then they escorted her down the aisle, singing a chant they had learned as a group, and for which they had written their own lyrics. The women developed new rituals for subsequent members' weddings. For Andrea's ceremony, they performed a spiral dance before the service. "The group led everyone in a grounding and called in the directions," Andrea recalls. "I stood in the middle, holding my mother's and my grandmother's hands as all of the women spiraled around us, forming a tighter and tighter knot, singing:

> *The river is flowing, flowing and growing*
> *the river is flowing down to the sea*
> *Mother, carry me, your child I will always be,*
> *Mother, carry me down to the sea.*

"It's now Reilly's sleep song," Ellie interjects, smiling. "She can't believe you all know the words."

"I remember," admits Andrea, "I was so nervous about our ritual being so exposed. But later my mother and my grandmother both told me that it was their favorite part of the ceremony."

As the women shared their group experience with their families, they developed a new respect for the power of the rituals they had created. That realization led them to open up even more, including their families in two annual celebrations they've crafted. Each May Day, they take out a maypole that they made their very first year. Standing nine feet tall, the pole is wrapped with colorful ribbons, which have never faded in all of that time. The women find a place of beauty in a regional park to lodge the maypole solidly into the ground, under the redwoods, and adorn it with spring flowers. "The park rangers all know us by now," Ellie says with a warm laugh. "They call us the maypole ladies."

The women ground and call in the directions. Then everyone, adults and children, takes hold of a piece of ribbon and, circling in both directions, weaves the ribbons together as they dance around the maypole and sing. Passersby stop to watch. After all the onlookers have satisfied their curiosity, the women and their families retreat to a potluck picnic.

The families are also included in a newer tradition, a fete for the winter solstice. The tradition began years ago before families were invited. Back then, the women would go to the beach. After dark they would build a fire and, completely naked, dance around the flames and swim in the bracingly cold ocean waters. The fire was used to purge the old and unwanted at year's end. "I remember," says Lisa, "I drew a picture of what I wanted to purge and threw it away, into the fire. You bring up the darkest stuff in your life and cast it off. You shed the burdens of the past." Now they call the ceremony their Festival of Lights. The women and their families form a circle, ground, have a meditation, and go around and say what they are each grateful for in the past year.

Over the years, as family responsibilities demanded more and more of their time, the group went through a rough patch, when meeting attendance waned.

"As we have grown older and our lives have changed, this sense of possibility, and the ritual, makes it worth leaving our families to be with the group."

After much discussion, the women decided to stop meeting every week and instead to meet one Tuesday and one Saturday a month. "It was a hard change to make," Ellie remembers. "The group had been so much about the weekliness, even the dailiness, of our lives, but now we realize the change has strengthened us. We had to be realistic about what we each could give."

The women have also struggled with the right balance between ritual and the more personal sharing time. They realized that at some point they had begun spending most of their group time on check-in. They recommitted to honoring ritual. "We decided that we wanted to be more conscious about bringing deeper energies into the group," explains Lisa, "because it makes for deeper connection." They returned to their original routine of having two people plan activities for each meeting, which had fallen by the wayside. "As we have grown older and our lives have changed," Lisa comments, "this sense of possibility, and the ritual, makes it worth leaving our families to be with the group."

Reexamination has led to a renewed level of commitment. To honor their sense of renewal, the women of the Fabulous Group designed a recommitment ceremony, held at the winter solstice a few years back, in celebration of their ten-year anniversary. "We invited everyone to dinner," Beth says. "All of our partners, our kids, even my mom came. We all lit candles. Because Laura was in many ways the initial spark for this group, she lit the first one. Then we each lit our family's candles."

clockwise from left foreground: Andrea, Beth, Lisa, Ellie, Megan, and Melanie

The women also drafted a group agreement, which they called the Seven Tenets of Commitment. That night they read the tenets out loud, and after each they said in unison, "We commit to this for the greater good of all":

1. We stand for a deeper sense of connection to ourselves, our community, and the spirit.

2. We recognize the importance of ritual as the central focus of our meetings. We agree to focus through "check-in," to ground, and to call in the directions each time we meet.

3. We come together on a regular schedule with the intention of creating a

structure, which allows us to nurture our goals, both together and individually. Our meetings are a retreat from the busyness of our lives, allowing us to step away from our daily responsibilities to a place that is both wider and deeper—a regular reminder that life is much bigger than our day-to-day concerns.

4. We recognize that familiar ritual is a gateway to our creative process and the expansion of inner exploration. We pursue concentrated, ongoing projects in which we create and explore together.

5. We celebrate the abundance of nature's beauty and the changes of the season with outdoor and seasonal rituals.

6. We include our families and our community, both with annual rituals such as May Day and the Winter Solstice, as well as by outreach to distant members. Once a part of the Fabulous Group, you are always part of the Fabulous Group.

7. We support each other through life's twisting, turning passages.

The women like to say that they "hold each other's wishes." "I feel like I want the best for everyone," explains Megan. "I am an extremely jealous and competitive woman"—she laughs—"but I don't feel it here. And I know that everyone holds my wishes." Melanie adds, "We've made that a priority in this group. What impacts one of us, impacts the others."

At another recent meeting, Ellie shared one such wish come true, a comfortable, quiet new home in a small community in Sonoma County, where she believes she can more easily raise her daughter on her own. Tacked on her kitchen wall, a sheet of paper reminds Ellie of what is important to her, and to the Fabulous Group:

In the end, these are the things that matter most:
How well did you love?
How fully did you live?
How deeply did you learn to let go?

—BUDDHA

That night, the women luxuriated in Ellie's wood-burning sauna, then let go of many things. Practicing the ritual they've come to love, they wrote down the things they wanted to purge from their lives, then threw the pieces of paper into a fire. They gave voice to what they wanted for the future.

left to right: Shirley, Ruth, Joy, Ruth, Florence, Judith, Mary

The Network

As the women of the Network will tell you, no one really prepares you for the disconnect between body and mind that comes with aging. You move through life, and then gradually realize that your body is beginning to betray you. You expect that part—that your joints will ache and your energy level will falter—but you don't expect that as your body declines, there is no corresponding decline in your intellect or your desire.

"In my heart, I don't feel old," confesses Ruth wistfully. Slim and striking at eighty, Ruth is the oldest but the most recent member of the Network. "There is a part of me back here"—she stabs a finger at the back of her head, raising thick, slate-colored hair—"that feels like an eighteen-year-old girl. A young girl with all of life ahead of her. And I don't think that will ever change."

But Ruth also vividly remembers what she calls her moment of truth. "I was fixing something at home as I always do. I was home alone and I went up on a ladder. Once I got up there, I realized I simply couldn't come down. My arthritis; my knee locked up on me." Ruth shakes her head in dismay. "I stayed up there, on that goddamn ladder, a very, very long time. And then finally someone came home and helped me down." As she tells her story, the women of the Network all laugh at her easy humor, but then slide into rumination, pondering their own moments of truth, when they knew that age was upon them.

"I had lots of ideas about what it would be like to get old. But it turns out that none of them are true," remarks Nancy. With cropped, barely graying hair and a warm, lively smile, Nancy is the baby of the Network at seventy-two. "This country values youth. So no one prepares you for what it's like to get old. You just move forward in ignorance, bumping along, fending for yourself. And that is the problem."

That is the problem. The women of the Network recognize that you enter advanced age with little information about all the indignities that will beset you. This is the reason the Network came together. When the group was conceived, most of the women were on the doorstep of senior citizenship.

For the past fifteen years, the seven women of the Network have been meeting the second Monday morning of each month, at Shirley's house. Confined to a wheelchair, Shirley is, in the minds of the others, the "heart" of the group. Her home boasts a side garden that spills onto the banks of the Hudson River. The dining room displays the exotic orchids she cultivates. The living room is crammed with books and artifacts from far-flung travels, with Danish modern furniture and framed art prints considered avant-garde when purchased decades before.

"I'm quieter in the company of men. I think it's important to be able to discuss these issues—very tender issues— just amongst us."

Joy was the one who came up with the idea for the group, to create a forum in which to discuss with candor the process of aging and the health issues it raises. "I remember there were some very basic medical issues that I wanted to discuss," she recalls, "like who was the best dermatologist in town to deal with the problems of aging skin. Or whether we continue seeing a gynecologist at our age."

Some of the women initially thought they should include their husbands, to have a couples roundtable on the issues of growing old together. But several were adamant that the Network be a women-only gathering. "I'm quieter in the company of men," admits Mary, who lost her husband several years ago. "I know that about myself. I think it's important to be able to discuss these issues—very tender issues—just amongst us."

"Yes," adds Ruth, "there is such an atmosphere of intimacy and trust here. There is an incredible honesty among these women. They all say what they really mean and think, they take risks. I always feel as if the things we discuss are confidential. I never worry that someone will repeat them to others, to our husbands."

"Especially because we sometimes talk about our husbands," says Joy with a quick laugh. "We have issues with our mates and with their failing health," she continues. "There are lots of things that happen now in our lives that we simply can't control. Like fading memories, and our decline in physical endurance. Our need for naps in the afternoon," Joy quips, playing lightly with the truth.

By any objective measure, the women of the Network are old; their average age is more than seventy-five. That age is beginning to show, at least in their hands, laid out in pairs on the dining room table around which they gather. Skeins of blue veins, raised and pulsing vulnerably. Fingers yielding to the burden of cranky joints. Yet these women project an image not of frailty but of a potent sense of vitality and sharp-minded curiosity.

Joy, at seventy-five, is a prominent freelance writer who lectures widely on issues of youth development and community schools. With her solid, athletic frame, she evokes the physical sense of a much younger woman. Nancy drives daily to Manhattan, where she teaches early childhood education at a graduate school. Over the years, most of the women have participated in community work and social protest. They maintain an active interest in the public schools, and their local superintendent often meets with them to learn how older people view the educational system. Each member of the Network is an active, accomplished woman who refuses to retreat into a condition of diminished expectation.

The Network women all live within a mile of one another in a verdant, jewel-like village just thirty-five minutes by commuter train up the Hudson River from New York City. At the time of the group's founding, some of the members were already good friends. Yet the Network's creation added a new and important dimension to their friendships.

"Just being able to unload those feelings, those worries about growing old, to share them and laugh about them sometimes, that is so valuable."

"Just being able to unload those feelings, those worries about growing old, to share them and laugh about them sometimes, that is so valuable," Shirley explains. "It's what brings me to this group again and again." By trading stories of the unexpected, often exasperating effects of aging, the Network women demystify the process for one another.

Following Joy's initial agenda, the women at first devoted their discussions entirely to the physical process of aging and how to cope with it. They raised questions and sought answers about how their bodies were changing in ways unforseen. "We've spent hours, literally hours, discussing straightforward information that was too embarrassing to discuss elsewhere, about the physical changes, the indignities," says Judith. Now seventy-nine, Judith is a prominent psychologist who has written extensively on substance abuse and its effects on families. She lost her husband, Frank, to Alzheimer's disease several years ago.

"We've discussed how our bodies are changing," she elaborates, "rearranging themselves, really. We've talked about things like thinning hair. Do you realize how much my hair has thinned over the past decade?" she asks as she pulls plaintively at a snow white, shoulder-length strand.

"Who realized that you would lose the hair under your arms as you age?" asks Nancy. "And your pubic hair gets softer and straighter, like you are becoming a child again. Does anyone know that before you get old?" These women have learned that the adage is true, growing old is not for the faint of heart. But they approach aging pragmatically, like any other challenge in life.

As their trust of one another grew through the years, the Network women moved on from the discussion of health issues to more personal things. "The hardest thing to accept about aging," Nancy observes quietly, "is how completely you become defined by age. You are no longer known by your successes and achievements. You are just old. It's unfair, the stereotypes you must fight. That makes admitting that you need to slow down even more difficult." The Network women often talk about how hard it is to admit that you can't keep up, for fear either of disappointing others or of being marginalized.

The women also discuss the unrealistic expectations—both their own and those of their children—that as grandmothers they will be selfless and endlessly giving, and they share their frustrations about how tiring their roles as grandmothers can be. "We talk a lot about the physical exhaustion and how it impacts our relationships with our families, with our grandchildren," remarks Joy. "Our children have no idea how old we really are. How tired we get sometimes."

"I remember just a few years back," recalls Mary, "I used to help my daughter out and take her kids for long stretches at a time. I just can't do it anymore. My youngest grandchildren are three and four years old. It is physically exhausting just to have them come for a short visit. I feel guilty because I can't help out the way I used to, but I just can't." Mary is seventy-three. Quiet-mannered and gentle, she has four children, eight grandchildren, and five great-grandchildren, many of whom live nearby. Every other weekend she has huge family gatherings, which she loves despite how tiring they are, and which other members of the Network often attend.

"My kids want me to go to the beach with them for a week," Mary says. "But I just don't want to go. There is so much work involved, making meals, dealing with wet towels. And sitting on the beach—the sunburn, the sand in everything. It's just no longer physically comfortable for me."

The physical demands of grandmotherhood are not all that vex the Network women. They also struggle with the assumption that other interests must give way to spending time with their families. "There are," Mary says, "eleven or twelve regular things I do." Mary wanted to be an actress in her youth, and she now participates in Monday-evening readings of James Joyce's *Ulysses* and attends a literature club, among many other activities.

In the end, stoicism reigns. Mary goes on her beach vacation. But being able to grouse candidly with these women helps Mary face her challenges with grandmotherly magnanimity.

The life history these women share is also a special source of solace for them. They have always been seekers—of information, of truth, of intellectual connection. At each stage of life they have claimed a position on the vanguard, redefining the roles and the rules for women. Nancy recalls reading Betty Friedan's early feminist classic, *The Feminine Mystique*, on the beaches of Long Island in 1966. "I was thirty-four or thirty-five at the time and the book really changed my life. I started to rethink completely what I wanted to do. I tore my world apart and turned it upside down."

Shirley recounts her experience as a young girl. "I was told by my middle-school teacher that I really shouldn't let boys know how smart I was." Paying no heed, she went on to serve in World War II and attend graduate school. Later she helped women prisoners obtain their GEDs, and taught Japanese women to

Joy and Ruth

speak English. "The rules have changed so dramatically since we were young," she says. "And we've experienced it all."

"We were all born long before the women's rights movement took hold," Nancy says. "When I was a teenager and went into the city, I had to wear white gloves and stockings and a hat—even when it was as hot as hell. Now I wear whatever I want when I teach in the city—such unbelievable changes in one little life." She adds with a proud smile, "I once rode an elevator with Eleanor Roosevelt." As young women, the Network members all shared an unbridled admiration for Eleanor Roosevelt, for her conviction and courage.

Stoicism, modesty, and forbearance are highly valued personal traits among this group. Children of the Depression, these women watched their parents deal with much hardship and loss. "I remember going to the bank with my mother in 1929, on the day the banks were all closed," recalls Ruth. "People were so frightened and angry."

Judith adds that when the stock market crashed, her stockbroker father called it "the death of Santa Claus." "The Depression was an equalizer," explains Ruth. "Everyone lost their jobs. I remember, even in the suburbs where we lived, beggars coming to the door."

The women also vividly recall the trauma of World War II. Each remembers with perfect clarity the day Roosevelt died. "Those experiences, the hardships we have seen, have certainly had an impact on the way we all have conducted our lives," says Joy. "They also affected our own consumption habits, our expectations in life."

The women often talk about how different life has been for their children and grandchildren. "They don't understand what it is like to do without," says Joy. "They don't understand hardship and deprivation. Kids these days just think that everything is disposable."

"Yes, exactly," adds another member with exasperation. "I am outraged by my grandkids' materialism, their attachment to material things. I just read an article in the *New York Times* about this new high-tech scooter, the latest rage. I'm sure my grandson will have a Razor scooter by the end of the week."

The group offers the women the opportunity to speak freely about these things without offending their families. Or of defying society's expectations of unfailing sweetness from older women. One member concedes, "Here we can be opinionated old women who speak our minds." Another member remarks mischievously, "All my daughter wants to talk about these days is her menopause. Well, I'm getting a little tired of her menopause." The women laugh.

Joy then raises another troubling expectation. "We talk a lot about our spouses, about their declining health and what it means for each of us. We've all had husbands who are in and out of the hospital. We talk about what it will be like to care for them, to deal with their physical failings when we are dealing with our own decline. What it will be like to be on our own."

"I joined this group when I turned sixty. . . . I had been racked with fears of isolation and loneliness. . . . Now I know I will never be lonely."

Mary especially recalls how helpful the group was after her husband passed away. "He had a heart attack, was in the hospital for about ten days, and then he just died. Shirley hosted a gathering at her home after the memorial service, and I remember being in her beautiful garden at the river's edge, surrounded by all of these lovely, loving women. It was so obvious to me how much these women respected and loved Frank. That knowledge helped me deal with my loss and with my life alone ever since."

In Judith's life, the Network played an important role as she dealt with her husband's progressive descent into the nightmare of Alzheimer's disease. "My husband was very ill for a long time and it was horrendous. It went on for years. His personality changed, his real self left him, and I was left dealing with this man, whom I felt I no longer knew, but who depended on me so deeply. Who needed me. I brought all of it to this group. My pain and fear and exhaustion. This group saved me. I never would have survived on my own."

Countering the isolation that so often befalls women in older age is a real source of power within the Network. "I joined this group when I turned sixty," Nancy says. "I thought it was such a wonderful idea because I had been racked with fears of isolation and loneliness. My friends were dying. I was afraid I would be left all alone. Now I know I will never be lonely." She adds thoughtfully, "It's a very powerful thing to be making new connections, to be deepening friendships at a time in your life when you had expected to withdraw from the world."

The women of the Network are growing old together, with fierce beauty. They are challenging stereotypes. They are facing down their fears with humor and support. They are taking matters into their own hands and redefining the process of aging. Judith discusses newfound love. Her eighty-six-year-old "boyfriend," Leonard, has recently moved in with her, and their relationship inspired her to start another group, called Late Life Links, a group of couples who discuss the complications posed by finding a new partner later in life. "There are so many issues," Judith explains. "My children, Leonard's children—they just don't know how to deal with us. There are issues of money and how to share your time with two different families. It is all so fascinating."

The latest Network gathering is at Shirley's house, where the lilacs in her side garden are in full bloom. Their meeting begins, as it often does, with a discussion of what was in the *New York Times* that morning. The women love contemporary affairs. In their conversations, the current political scene and the latest books get more time than geriatrics.

"In truth," Joy concludes, "though we started off by talking about health issues, our true bond is that of plain, quiet, gentle friendship." Ever in the vanguard, the Network women will continue to redefine what it means to be a woman at every stage of life.

left to right: Meg, Kay, Lilla, Leslie, Sandra, Frances, Ann, Nancy

The Company
of Women

Sometimes conflict among women is not a sign of things gone wrong. Sometimes it's an indication that things are right, that the women involved are brave enough and committed enough to speak in their truest voice. And if they speak truthfully and listen with intent—even in the scariest moments of confrontation—then a bond may result that is remarkably strong. This proved true for the Company of Women.

The group first came together in celebration of Leslie's forty-ninth birthday. Leslie invited a select group of her women friends for a weekend slumber party at her mountain cabin outside Asheville, North Carolina. "I wanted only the women I wanted at my birthday," she explains playfully. "I asked each of these women to come and to give me the gift of themselves and their friendship." They were a wonderfully diverse group. Among the eight are women in their thirties, forties, fifties, and sixties. There are six divorcees, one lesbian, and one woman who has been married for forty-five years. There is an independent filmmaker and a real estate agent, a lifelong homemaker and two therapists, a general contractor who builds luxury homes, a painter, and a dentist. They did not all know each other at the time, but their mix of personalities and interests blended beautifully. The women had a glorious time.

Leslie fondly recalls the delight of her birthday dinner that weekend. "I had set the table with earthenware goblets and blue-and-white plates, dusted with tiny stars which reflected the light. The women added beautiful mountain foliage they had gathered on their walks. It was magical."

The women spent hours and hours in their pajamas talking. Ann and Nancy, the gourmets among them, prepared the meals. The women hiked up Balsam Mountain to a cascading waterfall where, toes dipped in cool mountain water, they gave a blessing for Leslie. Reveling in the warmth they felt for each other, they committed to meet regularly for similar weekend retreats, and the group was born.

Only three gatherings later, however, their newfound vision of a women's group was threatened by long-pent-up tensions between Meg and Kay, two of its members who had been friends for years. It was April 1996 and the group was gathering at Sandra's vacation home, right next door to Ann's, in Point Clear, Alabama, on the eastern shore of Mobile Bay. With its clean but brackish water, the bay has long been a summer escape. Sandra's home, at water's edge, has floor-to-ceiling windows that open to the breeze. Mature oaks cast a cooling shadow over the wide porch that rims the house.

The women had arrived Friday afternoon, brimming with anticipation and eager to shed the stresses of their Atlanta lives. But by the time they sat down to their evening meal, tensions between Meg and Kay began to surface.

"We were all really beginning to settle in, to get comfortable with one another again. We were laughing and giggling like a bunch of teenagers. All except Meg," Kay recalls. "Throughout the evening, I kept feeling this intense negative energy from Meg. Whatever I said, whatever I did, it would just hit me. I could feel it. And I guess everyone else felt it too."

"It's true," Meg admits. "Kay and I had known each other for a long time— long before this group came together. And there were issues, old issues and resentments we hadn't resolved. Well, that night I was feeling excluded, like Kay was taking up the spotlight and deliberately leaving me out. It was a real teenage kind of feeling. Of not belonging."

The next morning, the women gathered for "check-in," as they always do, when each of them talks about what's going on in their lives. When it was Kay's turn, she immediately confronted Meg. "I can feel how mad you are at me," she said.

"And of course," recalls Meg, "I said I had absolutely no idea what Kay was talking about. I just denied it all," she admits somewhat sheepishly.

"Well, honey, it's understandable," Leslie adds in her Arkansas drawl. With her southern sensibility, Leslie knows how to put anyone at ease. "Women hate confrontation."

"But for whatever reason," Kay continues, "I just could not let it go." Her voice goes hot with dredged-up emotion. "I remember my face getting red. I started to cry and I said, 'I'm not going to let you get away with this, Meg. I can tell you hate my guts. Right now, you just hate my guts.'" That was the beginning.

As the story is recounted, the women let out a collective shudder. They are now gathered for a weekend in Aiken, South Carolina, to attend the opening of a multimedia exhibit produced by two members in honor of the group. They sit thigh to thigh on upholstered couches and wingback chairs in the sitting room of a Victorian guest house, dressed in sheer cotton or loose linen garments in concession to the muggy September morning.

"I had never experienced anything like it in my life, that degree of conflict. It was inordinately painful to watch," says Lilla, a much-sought-after Atlanta contractor whose life appears to be in complete order. "We all felt so threatened. We were shell-shocked. Here we had come together to connect and to hold each other close."

"Yeah," adds Sandra, running her fingers through her closely cropped hennaed hair. "I remember thinking to myself, This really sucks." She lets out a nervous laugh. "My first instinct, I think all of our first instincts, was to try to fix things. To separate Meg and Kay and get them to cool down and make up. But I think we all knew that it went deeper than that. That there was no easy answer to what was coming between them."

Instead of attempting to defuse the conflict, the six other women gave Kay and Meg the time and space they needed to work things out on their own. They left—fled, really—to Ann's home next door, where they spent a distracted afternoon puttering around the kitchen. But in taking their leave, the women made clear that they were not abandoning the two women locked in conflict.

"I remember saying to Meg and Kay," recalls Leslie, "'We hold this space for you. We are afraid of all of this, but we love you both. We want this group to endure. So please, please, work it out between you.' And then we left them alone."

Meg and Kay had been friends for many years, but in the several years before the group was formed, their friendship had faltered. "At one point," Kay explains, "we had been very close. Then I pulled back dramatically from the friendship. I really made myself unavailable to Meg, without explanation. And we never fixed that before we reconnected through this group."

"Our conflict had to do with our place within this group," Meg explains. There is about Meg a sense of fragility, of being haunted by her past. Her skin is ivory, her hair the color of palest cornsilk. Emotions play readily on the surface of her aquamarine eyes. "It was like I was back in high school. I felt like Kay was the cool girl, and I was the odd girl out. I felt like I didn't have a place to talk. Kay had pushed me away before, and now I didn't know if I belonged. I wasn't sure I felt safe in this group."

The feeling of not belonging, of otherness, had trailed Meg since childhood. She recalls the trauma of having moved to the South from Brooklyn as a young girl. Her dark-complected Italian mother, a Juilliard-trained opera singer, was ethnic and loud and dramatic—everything her South Carolina classmates' mothers were not. "I guess I was looking, through this group of women, for a sense of belonging which I hadn't found when I was young. And here was Kay, yet another diva, another drama queen in my life, threatening all of that and making me feel like an outsider again."

There was no quick fix to Meg and Kay's tensions. Over the course of a seemingly interminable day, they shouted at each other through tears, turned on their heels only to come together to shout again. "More than once," Lilla recalls, "when I checked in on Kay, I told her that I would take her home if she really needed to leave."

"And I said the same to Meg," adds Nancy. "But we all told them both that they needed to hear each other out, as painful as that might be. We told them to hold the vision of what our women's group might be if we survived all of this."

"So we just kept on talking," Kay recounts. "We ended up that evening sitting cross-legged on the floor, really close to one another. We were spent, really wrung out. But at some point we each began to really listen. I finally realized how much I had hurt Meg, and I apologized to her for how I had set such restrictive boundaries on our friendship."

Kay, as it turned out, had been holding back her own frustrations. "I also told Meg," she continues, "that there had been a long period in our earlier friendship when it seemed that I was always taking care of her. She had seemed so needy." As they settled into calm conversation, Kay told Meg that in order to be friends, Meg needed to be her equal, and that Kay could not be her caretaker. "We had to shift the balance of power between us," Kay recalls.

Through hours of speaking out with frightening candor, Kay and Meg cleared away old hurt and reignited their friendship.

When the tension lifted, the other women came out of hiding. Sandra recalls the sense of relief. "We all took a deep breath for the first time that day. We hugged and kissed because we all realized that our group had done something really brave. We knew we would be stronger for it." Sandra's face shines as she smiles. "It's funny, my cat Zack had cut out as soon as the sparks had started flying that morning. All day he was nowhere to be found. But by that evening, even Zack knew it was safe to come home."

"Whenever one of us feels disconnected or removed from the group, when we wonder whether it's all worth it, I always say—it's like a marriage. Sometimes all it takes is just showing up."

Many lessons were learned by all of the women in the course of that conflict. They learned about the sustaining power of group bonds, which can provide the structure and safety within which to repair and resurrect difficult friendships that might otherwise fade. They also experienced the deep sense of satisfaction that can arise when hurts and disagreements are bravely confronted and resolved. And they discovered the importance of each woman's commitment to the group dynamic. "Whenever one of us feels disconnected or removed from the group," Sandra says, "when we wonder whether it's all worth it, I always say—it's like a marriage. Sometimes all it takes is just showing up."

Reflecting back on that grueling day, Meg notes, "We did an amazing thing, really, we fought our tendency to flee. Many people—women—have not been trustworthy in my life. So I often have one foot out the door. With these women, I am learning trust. They are teaching me about a sense of steadfastness and continuity which the rest of my life has lacked."

Meg is not alone in her thoughts. "There were and still are within this group

Meg and Kay

real issues of distrust," Kay observes. "Many of us had come to associate female intimacy with danger and pain in our earlier lives. Being in this group has allowed us to reexamine those associations."

Frances reveals, "My childhood was quite painful. When I first joined this group, I was terrified to receive any sense of nurturing because I hadn't really experienced it before. And I feared that there was no way that I could reciprocate." Frances's face, a perfect heart shape, is attractively framed by her graying hair. As she speaks, she tucks short strands behind her ears. "These women have offered to me the highest ideals of friendship. They have been such a source of healing."

Most of the women had serious hesitations about the group at first. As Nancy recalls, "I had never been in a women's group before this. I don't have sisters, and I hadn't had any close female friendships, at least since high school. I associated female interaction with triviality, or worse. Negative things like jealousy. Backbiting. Competition. It took me a long time to get comfortable in this group, to open up. But these women have just rolled with me."

"Nancy is the group's turtle," Sandra offers affectionately. "She is quiet and steady and present. And close to the ground."

Nancy smiles broadly. "But once I allowed myself to trust these women, I found them to be such a tremendous source of strength. These are my three-o'clock-in-the-morning friends." Nancy clears the emotion caught in her throat and smooths her brown pageboy. "I divorced my husband after twenty-nine years. When my son got married in Park City, Utah, Lilla and Meg came with me to the wedding ceremony." Nancy's ex-husband had just remarried. With Meg and Lilla next to her, she was able to sit proudly in the front row of the tiny chapel, next to her ex and his new wife. "These women made me feel strong," Nancy emphasizes.

"Now Nancy is dating again. And we are all living vicariously, through her," Meg adds with a tender smile. "We are all really fierce about one another," says Sandra. "If someone is in a difficult spot, our instinct is to pluck them out."

The group has allowed many members to make important personal transformations. "There are, within this group, such moments of compassion," says Ann, a statuesque woman in her mid-sixties with regal bearing. She has been married to the same man for more than four decades. When she joined the group, Ann had spent her entire adult life as a homemaker and had never earned an income of her own. "I grew up in an era when a woman's choices were quite limited. I chose to become a homemaker and for a long time I was fulfilled in that role. But my kids are long grown and more recently I have struggled with it. Searching for a greater sense of purpose. I brought all of my pain to this group."

When Ann disclosed her anguish, the group listened hard. Lilla spoke up first. "Cook for me," she said quite simply. "You love to cook, so cook for me." Lilla, the general contractor, has little patience or time for cooking, and she welcomed Ann's assistance in feeding her family. For two years Ann delivered dinners to Lilla's home. "It opened up my life," Ann explains. "I found this niche, this vocation—and at my age. I have love in all of my food. Cooking is my greatest gift." At the age of sixty-three, Ann not only started earning an income for the first time, but also gained a sense of independence she had never known. She now serves as a personal chef to several families in Atlanta. "I never thought I would experience a peace that tran-

"We have supported each other through huge life transitions—changes in career, separation and divorce and reconciliation, moves to different parts of the country. There are so many incredible moments of being there for one another, moments that have tied us together like a knot."

scends all understanding," Ann muses. "But that is what these women have given to me."

"When we have separated from our husbands and have had nowhere to go," Sandra relates, "we have opened up our homes to one another. I always feel like I have seven other homes. We have supported each other through huge life transitions—changes in career, separation and divorce and reconciliation, moves to different parts of the country. There are so many incredible moments of being there for one another, moments that have tied us together like a knot."

"Whenever we get into jams of misunderstanding or disharmony within the group," Sandra adds, "we just bring into memory those individual moments. Those dyad moments. And we know the group will survive."

A key to this group's intense bond is the fact that, in gathering, the women spend an extended period of time with one another, often far away from their individual homes. While the women all once lived in Atlanta, a few have now relocated along the Eastern seaboard. Their diaspora not only limits the frequency of their weekend retreats—typically only once every three to four months—but also forces them to put away their individual lives and concentrate on the group when they do meet.

"If we were to meet in Atlanta, those of us who live there would just 'do our Atlanta lives,'" Sandra observes. "Nancy, our real estate agent, would always have her ear to the phone. We would be drawn away by our partners and our families. So, even though many of us do often get together for a Friday-night dinner in Atlanta, we try to plan our weekends in spots far from home." The Company of Women has met in the warmth of Mobile Bay, on the sunny, sandy coast of South Carolina, in the deeply forested beauty of the Piedmont Mountains, in the pristine winter whiteness of Jackson Hole, Wyoming.

A weekend retreat also heightens the sense of celebration about their get-togethers. "We can do parties," Leslie pronounces with authority. They cook gourmet meals, wander city streets together, or simply lounge in the sun; whatever their mood inspires. One weekend at her cabin, Leslie brought in a massage therapist.

"Sometimes we never seem to get out of our pajamas," says Kay.

"Even Lilla," Meg adds with a laugh. Lilla, by her own admission, is a loner, someone who loves to work and travel and stay busy. "At first it was hard for me in this group," Lilla explains, "because often we do nothing. We just talk. About our work, our families, our challenges, and our dreams. Important stuff. But sometimes, I have a hard time staying put. I've learned, though. I've learned to put in my pajama time."

"Yeah," Frances adds. "Our style is 'in your jammies and in your face.'"

Good thorough conversation is at the core of every retreat. "We may spend Friday night just chatting or sharing photographs or stories," observes Sandra, "but by Saturday morning check-in, we are ready to put aside our public faces, what we show to the world, and get real with one another." During check-in the women will go methodically around the room, making sure each woman has had the chance to fully speak. And however long it takes to listen to each member's story is precisely how long the group will take.

"We challenge one another," Frances observes. "We have all been willing to go to a really deep place to find our authentic selves. We have all said, in the presence of one another, that we are going to be who we were meant to be."

These women bestow upon each other an unshakable sense of belonging in the face of their differences. "I am a lesbian," Frances says. "I have known that for most of my life, but it took me a long time to come out publicly. This group was so essential to my sense of self-acceptance." During a retreat to Myrtle Beach a few years back, she experienced a breakthrough. "The trip meant a lot to me," she explains, "because every summer as a child I would go to Myrtle Beach with my grandparents.

clockwise, from far left: Ann, Leslie, Sandra, Lilla, Kay, Nancy, Frances, Meg

"Well, there we were one night," she continues, "all of these women piled in my big car. We had the radio turned way up. We were cruising the main drag along the beach and singing beach tunes. You know, the Drifters, 'I Heard It Through the Grapevine,' that kind of stuff.

"We were coming up on this big, cheesy beach store on the boardwalk called The Gay Dolphin. Eight stories of green glass, right next to the saltwater taffy factory. It's a real tourist trap, filled with beach umbrellas and little souvenir people made out of seashells. I had seen that store year after year throughout my childhood.

"Well, that night it suddenly hit me," she recalls with a storyteller's flare. "The Gay Dolphin. The *Gay* Dolphin. It was sending me a message. I rolled down my car window and shouted at the top of my lungs to all the passing tourists, 'I'm gay! I'm gay! I'm gay!'

"Well, these women were all in my car, howling, rolling on the floor with laughter. And I was laughing too. It was a hysterical moment but it was a turning point. I was really outing myself." The other women in the group knew about Frances's sexuality and were comfortable with it, but as she recalls, "It was the first time in my life that I felt totally accepting of my own sexuality. And it's because these women make me feel so safe. And they each accepted me."

Each of the women, in turn, can tell a story of how the Company of Women has transformed her life. Leslie has found the encouragement to devote herself to her painting. "This group made me realize that art was my big healer," she recounts. "One day when we were all up in the mountains together, when I was just starting out as a painter, Kay encouraged me to bring my art to a show where she was selling her painted furniture. Well, I did. And I didn't sell a damn thing of course, not one piece." She reaches over and lays a hand softly on Kay's cheek. "But that was the first time I showed my work publicly."

Subsequently Lilla commissioned Leslie to design a logo for her contracting business, and all of the women have bought a painting by Leslie and have hung them in their homes.

Sandra has found the inspiration to write when she is with the group. "I am always at my most creative when I am with these women," she says. "That's when my muse calls on me, at 4:00 A.M., urging me to get up and write. My muse told me that I have a single responsibility and that is 'Always write stories that hold people large.' It is with her voice that I speak about these incredible women and it is through her eyes that I see them so truly." Sandra's nighttime writing resulted in a poignant collection of tales about the Company of Women, told in the manner of Native American myth, which she calls medicine stories.

Creativity begets creativity. These stories inspired Leslie to paint a series of watercolors illustrating them. The stories and paintings are combined in the exhibit opening at the Aiken Center that the women have gathered to celebrate. The exhibit will travel to several cities along the East Coast.

Sharing Sandra's medicine stories and Leslie's deeply revealing portraits with the public is an act of courage not only for the writer and artist but for each woman portrayed. Much is revealed in word and form: moments of dislocation and struggle. And of not belonging; of lacking a sense of place. But these portrayals of vulnerability and growth are relayed with tenderness. A central medicine story tells of the group's genesis, of that first weekend that brought them together in a cabin facing Balsam Mountain:

After Otter Mother had been fifty years in the village she called seven
  of the most wise.
Seven of the most fair,
Seven of the most loved
women of the principal people to her lodge for her birthday celebration.

The seven women brought love offerings to celebrate Otter Mother's birth. They laughed and wrapped their strong woman arms around each other as they vowed that day to create a circle of women—a whole much greater than the sum of its parts.
A circle that would honor, support and love the great spirit of women everywhere!

It was a very good day. Ho. *

---

*From *Medicine Stories for the Company of Women*, by Sandra VanPelt Hogue.

front row, from left: Leona, Colleen, Shea, Marcy, Mary; *back row, from left:* Mary, Valerie, Susan, Kathleen, Celeste, Susan

The Study Group

Were still all furious, outraged. It was just rich, very hot and passionate. We had examples of every kind of oppression. We didn't talk about our husbands, it was about women," explains Mary, one of the original and long-standing members of the Study Group. "That's why we kept coming back."

Women forge allegiances based on many commonalities—sometimes the frivolous or the personal, and at other points in life, the political and the serious. The Study Group was founded in the early 1980s as an outgrowth of activism, the ten early members seeking a serious course of in-depth study.

They felt a keen sense of purpose, the feeling of being on the cusp of something important. The country had come through a tumultuous era of protest focused on civil rights and the Vietnam War. Women were often on the sidelines, supporting the work of men. Quietly, though, many women were organizing around peace and social justice due to concern over the impact of nuclear arsenals on their children. The women's movement was emerging. The call for nuclear disarmament, marked by rallies, protests, and civil disobedience in the late 1970s, continued to mount in the early 1980s.

"Vietnam was over, but war wasn't over. War was still fresh in our minds," notes Janice, another founder of the Study Group. "There was the power of the sixties; we really believed that the revolution was around the corner—this was the next phase. It wasn't just about women, it was about life, and sustaining life—and demanding that people be able to live."

Many of the Study Group women first met in Seneca Falls, New York, as visitors to the women's Peace Encampment. The birthplace of women's suffrage, Seneca Falls was, in the 1980s, home to an encampment focused on nuclear disarmament. "We came home inspired," Marcy remembers. "We held weekly vigils against nuclear arms at home in Michigan." "And," Janice adds, "there were a lot of demonstrations going on near Detroit, at Walled Lake." Williams International in Walled Lake was at the time the sole supplier of the engines for cruise missiles. The protestors would go early in the morning, before their day jobs started, to demonstrate.

"As a woman I always felt marginalized in political movements. In the peace movement, it was considered a defection to talk about women. This group was how we made sure we had a voice."

This activism inspired the group's first "call to women." Janice, Marcy, Mary, Jeanette, Shea, and a few others, most of them teachers or social workers, were propelled by a sense of urgency to examine the role of women in social change movements. Janice remembers, "We were trying to find our voice, to answer the question, What is our role as feminists who are compelled by broader social justice issues?"

"As a woman I always felt marginalized in political movements," Kathleen recalls. "In the peace movement, it was considered a defection to talk about women. This group was how we made sure we had a voice."

When this core group decided to invite other women to discuss their work, ideas, questions, and hopes, they had no idea they were starting a women's study group that would last for decades.

Jeanette's home at the time was the ideal setting, a loft in the heart of struggling downtown Detroit. Janice remembers, "It had a huge bathroom decorated with two couches and all sorts of hip-looking mannequins. We held entire meetings in that bathroom." Not too far from where the other women lived, Jeanette's home was just right to open up to women across the city.

Jeanette and Janice both liked a notice they had seen at Seneca Falls, and borrowing from that they posted flyers that read, "Listen to Women for a Change." They had no idea how many women would come.

Shea, who had just finished her dissertation on stereotypes of women in the mass media, spoke at that first group forum on the history of the women's movement. The place was packed, and the evening was charged. After her presentation, the women broke up into small discussion groups. "We found," Shea says, "that we just couldn't talk enough to one another." So the evening turned into a series of forums, each with a topic and speaker.

Listen to Women for a Change...II took on the subject of the controversial deployment of cruise missiles, highlighting the work being done by the peace movement in Europe. Janice had spent a week at the Greenham Common Peace Camp in England and remembers, "Seneca was invigorating, powerful, but didn't compare to what was going on in Greenham." A U.S. Air Force base, Greenham Common was scheduled to receive nearly one hundred cruise missiles. Beginning in 1981, women lived and protested outside the base entrance. On December 12, 1982, thirty thousand women and men from across Western Europe linked arms to completely "embrace" the base; many women participated in a mass civil disobedience the next day. Janice met a mother from Detroit who took her two daughters to the demonstration and to visit the Peace Camp; she invited her to speak at the Detroit forum about her experience and the movement as seen through the eyes of her daughters.

The audiences for Listen to Women for a Change grew steadily and the venues changed. All the topics were political in nature, all in the spirit of learning and coalescing around social justice.

The energy generated by this series of forums precipitated the Study Group. Janice remembers, "A few of us, mostly the women who organized the forums, wanted more rigorous study on nonviolence and women. We were questioning our role as feminists moving into other areas of social justice. So, every other week we held potlucks, and one or two of us were in charge of readings and discussion." The women selected books to inform their debates and probe difficult questions. "I remember craving this," Janice says. "It was like our university."

Part of the reason for the Study Group was to work through more difficult books. "I remember," Janice recalls, "we read *Reweaving the Web of Life*, about feminism and nonviolence. We thought it would take us a few evenings; instead we spent a year and a half on this book. Each piece was so powerful." Deborah, a social worker who met the others demonstrating at Walled Lake, reflects, "When it was my turn to lead the discussion, it was scary and hard. People all took it so seriously."

Shea is gratified about how much she learned in those days about nonviolent action and theory. "The Study Group transformed me," she says. "I was a 'bomb thrower,' and now I am appalled by that." Those lessons now influence the way she works with children. Shea, who for years has run a summer program for inner-city kids, explains, "When I deal with a kid who is difficult to control, I call on an image from one of the first books we read. It was about a woman who was ready to smash a kid. But she turns around and simply touches his cheek and strokes it."

The women started out with a wide range of perspectives. Shea was the radical, a Marxist. Jeanette was from a Quaker family and brought that vantage to the group. "I came from a working-class background," Colleen says. "The whole idea of studying a book was just eye-opening." "And I," adds Deborah, "came to the group for study but found myself wanting to discuss more personal things. I was thirty-five and single and like that *Cathy* cartoon: 'Whoops, I forgot to have children.'" But many common experiences joined the women. "Rape, job discrimination," Mary remembers. "We all had examples of every type of oppression. We lived them." Kathleen, for example, was a flight attendant for a major airline, and she lost her job when she married. She became embroiled in a class action suit to challenge discrimination in the airline industry.

At first the women kept organizing the larger forums, even as the Study Group evolved. "We were very proud of what the group was—the force that it had in the Detroit area because of the larger forums we held. They were the mainstay of the Detroit women's community," says Janice. Sadie, a sociology professor and an African American, used her contacts to arrange an evening with four black women activists, as a way to bridge activism between black and white women in the peace movement.

One of the most powerful larger forums featured a member of the Jane Collective in Chicago. This feminist group offered abortions to women prior to the 1973 Supreme Court decision in *Roe* v. *Wade*. The night's discussion probed the complexities of the abortion issue, acknowledging that it wasn't cut-and-dry. Some women, offended, got up and left.

Their silent departure stimulated weeks of debate within the Study Group. "We had this very hard discussion," remembers Janice, "about how, even though women must have the right to choose to have an abortion, it is an emotional experience. We discussed the hard part, the regret. In some feminist communities it was taboo to talk about this, but it was real. We never strayed from our commitment to talk about the hard stuff. We talked about how you acknowledge the complication of choices. What this group helped us do was to keep paying attention to things you wouldn't otherwise pay attention to."

As the group became closer, tension developed. "It was almost against the rules to have a good time," Kathleen remembers. "We were so serious." Some members wanted to share more personal aspects of their lives, while others found intellectual conversation itself to be very intimate. Mary, now seventy-one, was the director of the Women's Center at Oakland College for years. She remarks, "When you talk about intimacy, for me it was sharing in a conscious way what political life meant, and it was such an important thing to be taking ourselves seriously as women."

"When you talk about intimacy, for me it was sharing in a conscious way what political life meant, and it was such an important thing to be taking ourselves seriously as women."

Shea was the least willing to give in to discussion of personal issues and she would get mad at the others for being "bourgeois." She had them read books on Marxism and class analysis. "I thought spirituality was for middle-class women with nothing better to do." But as she got to know several women in the Study Group who were intellectually rigorous and politically astute, and who nonetheless embraced spiritual issues, her views changed. Yet the sharing of the personal remained a struggle. Deborah often said to Shea, "I didn't ask you what you thought, I asked you what you felt."

Kathleen in particular pushed the group into intimate terrain. "In my own life," explains Kathleen, "I was facing something very important. I wanted to share it with the group but I didn't think it was allowed. We were a study group. But at the same time, these were the women I felt closest to." Kathleen had given her daughter up for adoption. She became desperate to find her, just to make a connection and know that she was all right, but she had exhausted all her resources and was encountering only dead ends.

"I dragged these women kicking and screaming to a more personal place," Kathleen says fondly. "I felt compelled to say more personal things. So we started, 'What's on tap?'" The Study Group women began to pass an egg timer, and everyone got three minutes to talk about their own life. If you needed more time, you were allowed. "We would get things off our chest, and then we could be more present. Then we could focus on study."

Before long, this part of the evening became as vital as the study. Struggles at work and at home were all "on tap." Marilyn's father got sick, then Shea's. "We had to find a way to cope with it all," Shea remembers. "Marilyn wrote a book on loss, which was how she coped with the sorrow. She included three of our stories in her book, and that helped all of us deal with the grief. She was such a wise woman." Celeste was struck by how much they learned from each other personally and politically, revealing, "I learned to take myself seriously, listening to the reverence with which everyone's issues were handled. It was powerful, sacred."

The group also invented rituals of support and celebration as it matured. "I was one of the first members of the Study Group to get pregnant, I may have been the first," recalls Janice. "The Study Group tried something new, they made me a Blessing Way. So much of our work had been about reproductive health, and here we were welcoming new life. We were coming together around something bigger than us." The house was transformed, candles burned on the fireplace ledge; purple and blue flowers were everywhere, iris and daisies, and there was food. Janice's most vivid memory is of Deborah. "I remember her rubbing cornmeal on my feet, to connect me with the earth." The women also presented Janice with a quilt they had made. Each woman made a piece of it, and Marcy sewed it together. All the pieces were symbolic; one was a woman in a circle, to

Marcy, Celeste, and Kathleen

portray civil disobedience. "It was one of those 'you never forget' moments of your life," Janice recalls. "It was deeply moving. I had a sense of being comforted and held by these women."

After the baby was born, Jeanette organized the women to cook meals every day for three or four weeks. The group had become an integral part of each other's lives. The Study Group women then instituted a tradition of "Blessing Ways" for each member who became pregnant. Valerie, who had worked with Janice for ten years at a teen center, remembers her "feminist baby shower." "I was naked, in a room filled with candles. Every member brought something to read. But mostly, it was a physical experience. The other women massaged my body and talked about what they hoped for my child. Then they gave me gifts, for me, not my baby. It was the most attention I got as an individual, not just as the mother of my baby."

The Study Group has performed many such rituals through the years, celebrating family events. One of their favorites was the ceremony they held for Jeanine's child, Choi. Jeanine and her husband adopted Choi from Korea. When Choi began menstruating her parents asked if she would like to celebrate her coming of age with friends. Choi, responding like most preteen girls, said that it would be embarrassing. But then she thought about it and said to her mother, "If I could come to your group, that would be all right—if your women's group wants to celebrate, that would be great." All the women in the Study Group brought Choi small gifts and flowers. "We all told stories about getting our own periods. I was struck by how no one of our generation had celebrated it, in fact, someone said her mother told her how sorry she was for her," Susan remembers. The women ended the evening by toasting Choi's womanhood with cherry juice.

The group has also endured the loss of several members, whom they helped face death. Sadie, one of the original members, was diagnosed with cancer. "She was such an inspiration," reflects Marcy. "She was so humble. Whenever we would get stuck on some really esoteric point, Sadie would bring us back down to earth." Towards the end of her life, Sadie returned to her hometown of Pontiac, Michigan, to buy a square foot of land in a neighborhood where blacks had not been allowed, just to make a point. To comfort her in her illness, the group created what they called a healing circle. Sadie came to a group gathering and they massaged her unclothed body. Deborah is struck by the memory of it. "It is one of my most powerful images of the group, to be so close and intimate, to massage someone's body, and then never to see them again. It was very sad. But holy."

"Our movement toward spirituality epitomized the wholeness of it, of who we had become. The polarities were joined; our political work and our spiritual work. We were all growing together."

"Our movement toward spirituality epitomized the wholeness of it," Marcy observes. "Of who we had become. The polarities were joined." "It was like circles interlocking," concludes Kathleen. "Our political work and our spiritual work. We were all growing together."

Through its many years, the Study Group has lost many members but has endured by welcoming new ones. The group recently hosted a reunion of all of its members, both old and new. Kathleen took that opportunity to finish a story that she began telling the women almost two decades ago. "I found my daughter. She finally called. She didn't want to be contacted at first, but then she called on her birthday—August 9. She was turning thirty-three. She thought it would be a treat for me. We talked for a few hours. I now know that she is safe and happy, living alone and working. I feel totally healed by the experience. I keep my heart open."

Mary reflects on the Study Group's ability to re-create itself. "While in the early years there was so much urgency of purpose, the group has mellowed in more recent years. We've come to a place where peace and reconciliation are the goal," Mary concludes. "It's a deeper but equally powerful place where women's groups are today."

clockwise, from lower right: Carol Jo, Nancy, Kathy, Marlaina, Lynn Ann

The Yoga Circle

The Yoga Circle has a lot of power to it," Marlaina observes. "There is a lot about being in the moment with yoga. You don't dredge up the past, you don't live in the future, you live in the moment; that is what you have. In the yoga discipline, every time you're in the past or in the future, you gently guide your body, yourself, back to the present. Our circle exemplifies this."

Thursday evening at 7:30, six women are convened on Carol Jo's carpeted living-room floor. Her comfortable one-story East Lansing house looks similar to many on her block. This Midwestern town is home to a large land-grant university and has the ease of a small town coupled with the intellectual stimulation a university tends to foster.

Each in loose and comfortable clothes, the women sit cross-legged, ready to experience what the evening will bring. The living room is lined with wooden shelves stuffed with books. Carol Jo takes musical instruments from a deep wicker basket and piles them in the center of the floor: two bells—one with a black stem, the other gold-stemmed—tambourines, cymbals, drums, and rattles. Several lighted candles sit on a carefully composed altar that is covered in a bright red cloth. One member who brought cider and a nut mixture finds a place for it on the floor. Carol Jo's two cats are stretched out; they are in regular attendance.

The women sit up straight and close their eyes. Hands resting gently in their laps, each curves her thumbs and index fingers together, forming a relaxed circle. This is a yoga tradition that helps energy flow throughout the entire body, according to Eastern theory. The Western interpretation tells us that placing one's fingers together creates a conditioned response; if one meditates in this position, and then later simply places one's fingers together, relaxation settles in.

Posture in place, an evening for the Yoga Circle always begins with a chant, a rhythmic repetition of words or sound to induce calm. There are many different chants—English, Indian, fast, slow. "The chant brings you into meditation," Carol Jo explains. "Usually we use Sanskrit words. The goal is to tune in to the sound and the feeling, to shut out your mind, all the static—to diffuse the day. It has a centering effect."

The Yoga Circle was ahead of its time. These women began practicing yoga thirty years ago. "'Yoga' means union, bringing people together, which is what we do," Lynn Ann notes. "We have a sort of 'shared language' because of yoga," Marlaina adds, agilely adjusting her body. "It is a discipline. We have all learned the same breathing techniques and the importance of body movement. Yoga pulls you back to your core. Most every morning I do yoga stretches that we learned together as a group. I've done it for years now. They tone my body. The sun salutation is my favorite." "Everyone tries to do some yoga every day," remarks Carol Jo. "But with the group, at least once a week we can count on attending to the spiritual and to our bodies."

Unlike most women's groups, this one has thrived on open membership. Over the years many members have found their way to the Yoga Circle through yoga classes or word of mouth. "Anyone can come," explains Carol Jo, "but there is a core of four to six of us who are really involved." The group was started by Carol Jo's yoga teacher, and at that time it was strictly about doing yoga, more like a class. Over time, many of the original group members moved away, and most of the current core group joined twenty years ago. In order to attract new members, the circle occasionally hosts "yoga Sundays," with breakfast, which are publicized to the community.

All members can come as often or as infrequently as works for them. "What is special," says Marlaina, "is that you can come every week or not come for five years and there is a sense that wherever you are on your journey, you are embraced. How lucky we are to be able to fold in and out of this group as we each need to." "Even the people who don't show up keep in touch," Carol Jo remarks softly. "This group has been my family," she adds, "meeting with the same people, many of the same people most every week."

"What is special is that you can come every week or not come for five years and there is a sense that wherever you are on your journey, you are embraced."

For years the group had a leader, Mamar, and always met at her home. When Mamar became ill with cancer, she no longer had the energy to lead, but she still wanted the group to gather at her home. After Mamar died, they decided not to have a leader anymore. "It has made us more creative, not having a leader," says Peg, one of the long-standing members.

The group began because of yoga, but now do many other activities. The women always start by chanting, and most often do yoga. They also meditate, doing either silent or guided meditation, and sometimes someone will bring a spiritual reading or a video for the group to discuss. "We experiment with new activities, like healing techniques and polarity circles," Peg explains. "We will try anything anyone wants to share or learn about. We are always open to new influences."

Peg and Sharon are interested in chakras, so they have taught the group about them. Peg and yet another member, Kathy, have started studying esoteric healing, and Kathy is practicing what she's learned on the animals she treats in her veterinary practice. "Many people are surprised at how we make decisions," Peg describes. "No one votes; someone presents an idea and it evolves. Sometimes we are not even sure a decision has been made, but then we find ourselves in the middle of what was proposed."

Unlike many groups, the Yoga Circle does not devote much time to discussing what's going on in the members' lives. "The way we know each other is not necessarily by the details of life," explains Peg. "We don't always talk about details, sometimes your mind just wants a shift." Instead these women have fostered intimacy through the yoga itself. While for some, yoga is primarily about toning one's body, for many, the yoga poses help release trauma or pain that has been stored for years. Yoga helps let go of past hurt that has been held in one's muscles, stored as body memories.

This group is more intuitive than intellectual. "We bring our challenges here because it is an opportunity to transform the issue," Peg continues. "It is not a matter of problem-solving." Kathy responds, "It's a more healing energy. When my mother was dying, I was in a lot of pain. I am not sure how it happened but I just lay down on the floor and all of these women kind of held me. It was like an energy circle." She pauses. "There is a real sensitivity in this group."

"The Yoga Circle is 'an allowing' atmosphere," observes Lynn Ann. "Last spring when my husband had a tumor, I felt like I could hold it all together all week and then Thursday night it would be safe to cry and scream and be who I was. The Yoga Circle provided a different kind of support than even my family gave me. They didn't tell me how I should feel, they didn't tell me how I shouldn't feel. I always felt completely unjudged."

One experience that created a new closeness in the group was the death of their onetime leader Mamar. "When Mamar was dying of cancer I took care of her," Lynn Ann recounts. "It was a degree of intimacy I have never known with anyone." At the Thursday meeting the week before Mamar died, the group gathered around her and sang to her. To ease her pain, they carried her outside to be in nature. "All of us loving her so much," Carol Jo says, "we became even more bonded."

The respect the women feel for one another, and the satisfaction the group brings them are readily evident. "There are a lot of strengths and resources within the group," Peg says. "We are women of many dimensions." She describes one of their favorite activities. "Every so often Marlaina treats us to her storytelling. I remember the evening she brought beautiful, vibrantly colored scarves and used them to illustrate the wonderful stories she tells from around the world. We were all mesmerized."

"I've always been a seeker," Marlaina interjects. "What is our purpose on earth? How can we embrace it? So I try to act on that. It seems I try a new thing every ten years," she laughs. "In the sixties it was the peace movement. In the seventies it was alternative health. That turned out to be a mistake," she says with chagrin. "All three of my daughters rebelled against it. In the eighties, it was expanded consciousness, and the nineties was storytelling. I'm still storytelling, but now I write songs, too. I always felt there were other dimensions to life and other worlds, so I've been obsessed with self-growth and getting rich in experience. It was in the eighties, my era of expanded consciousness, that I discovered yoga and our circle."

Kathy, whose life by day as a veterinarian is a great contrast to Marlaina's, responds, "We're all seekers, coming from our own highest good. What we create together is greater than each of us individually. Perhaps this sense of unconditional acceptance and love makes the group like a 'container'—we're not gossipy, we're very confidential."

"People sometimes stereotype women like us," admits Marlaina. "But we are not flaky, wispy types. We are hard-nosed women, women who are strong in the marketplace."

Peg, a nutritionist who moved to East Lansing from Washington, D.C., in the late seventies, found the group to be an anchor when she arrived. "It was tough getting connected in East Lansing. I had been so involved in the peace movement and civil rights in D.C. and came to East Lansing kind of burned out. I had just left my marriage and had no children. If there was an unpardonable sin in those days, it was divorce. I felt as if I had been bad, as if the gods would be vengeful toward me. The Yoga Circle offered me a way to connect to something larger than myself. It connected me spiritually in a different way."

Lynn Ann spends her weekdays working for the State of Michigan as the director of migrant education. She says, "The group is a safe place to be who you are. If something touches your heart or makes you think during the week, you bring it to the group. It is a nice sounding board for people interested in alternative spiritual ideas—there is no judgment. And now, because there is no leader, we may just sit in silence for a while. As we grow and mature, the structure is not as important to us."

"We are capturing the force of the feminine. We are all trying to be more feminine in a powerful sense, and the yoga moves reinforce this. The feminine has great power."

Smiling, Peg adds to Lynn Ann's thoughts. "It is a feminine energy group. Even when men have visited, they show their feminine energy. It is nurturing, more circular in structure, and nonhierarchical."

clockwise, from lower right: Nancy, Carol Jo, Kathy, Lynn Ann, Marlaina

"We are capturing the force of the feminine," Marlaina reflects. "We are all trying to be more feminine in a powerful sense, and the yoga moves reinforce this. The feminine has great power, endurance, and practical applications to life."

"But," Peg says with a sly smile, "we have our edges. If we feel like we are being too goody two-shoes, we'll all say, 'Let's get down and dirty.'" "Yes," agrees Marlaina. "We can be humorous and bawdy at times."

While yoga instructs one to be in the present, the Yoga Circle uses the New Year as an opportunity for life assessment. Lynn Ann explains, "Every New Year we have our angel party and we talk about the past and the future, our own and each other's." These celebrations started years ago, before angels became of popular interest. This year the invitation reads:

Calling all angels, come join with your fellow angels for an evening of angelic activities, sing angel songs, tell angel stories, do angel meditations, bask in the glow of the spirit of angels, right here on earth!! And of course draw your new angels for the coming year—don't start the New Year without them!!!

The party is lively and festive. There is a delicately crafted "angel altar." Candles are lit everywhere, and someone will make angel food cake. Everyone who has ever been connected with the Yoga Circle gets an invitation. "Even some of the husbands come and have their spirits touched by the angels," one woman says with a laugh.

The highlight of the evening is when the women draw three new angel cards for the year to come. Angel cards come in a packaged series; each circular card is illustrated, with an angel, of course, and has one word of significance or wisdom. The words are open to interpretation and are intended to inspire reflection: *Light, Balance, Grace, Humor, Creativity, Power, Adventure, Abundance, Flexibility, Tenderness, Delight, Gratitude.*

The women sit and discuss how their angel cards from the year just ended were reflected in the events of the year, and then contemplate the significance of their new cards. "Last year I got the card of *Power,*" Marlaina recalls, "and sure enough all last year I was dealing with the issue of power. I realized that I often give my power away and hadn't appreciated the extent of my own power. This year I drew *Transformation, Connection,* and *Work.* There is a sense of courage and awe, looking at our lives together."

"When we talk about our angel cards, I can see how I've grown over the year," observes Lynn Ann. "And other people see things I don't—or reasons why certain cards are relevant to my life. I might not see any experiences that relate, but others might. We let go of last year and embrace the New Year."

Reflecting on the personal growth the group has inspired, Carol Jo comments, "We are a community of souls on journeys." The women all feel that they have become more fully themselves through the support of the group. Some of the women have been profoundly transformed, such as Carol Jo. "I was extremely timid, for years," she says. "I came to the Yoga Circle and I didn't talk." "And now you've become fierce!" Marlaina interjects. "In the best sense of the word."

Peg considers her own transformation. "I've always been out there in the world, involved in movements and activities. This group has made me focus on my inner life. I'm evolving into an introvert." There are tears in her eyes. "I'm not comfortable with it yet, this new person inside me. But it is a rich journey."

Much personal growth behind them and still more ahead, enjoying their toned and strengthened bodies, the women of the Yoga Circle assess where they want to go next. "We are pioneers in a sense," reflects Marlaina. "The world has to shift. There has to be more bounce, more of a spiritual element. Let's be wilder, let's be more passionate." Marlaina concludes, "Perhaps we'll get up early, go out into nature, see the sunrise, and do our yoga. Perhaps we can be freer."

back row, from left: Judy, Nedra, Kay, Barbara; *front row:* Ann, Sue

The Birthday Group

Thursday, June 22. Today Nedra will turn sixty, and the women of the Birthday Group will gather in her honor.

Kay has planned a birthday luncheon for Nedra at the Ada Country Club. A proper table with stiff ironed linens is being set along the picture windows of the Club's main dining room. The windows offer an expansive view of the pool and the golf course just beyond. It is a lovely place for a celebration. Even Barbara, struggling with illness, refuses to miss it. She rose at 5:00 A.M., making her way to the Ada Clinic for her dialysis, so that she could be here at noon with her friends.

The women of the Birthday Group are all firmly rooted in Ada, Oklahoma. Most were born here, have raised their children here, have spent their entire lives here. Ada is a full two hours' drive from Oklahoma City, with no easy access to the interstate. Main Street leads into town, past Black Angus farms, oil wells—some rusted, some pumping rapidly—a city park, and Dicus Markets, owned by one of the members, Ann, and her husband. Ada is a small, quiet place. But through their group gatherings and inspired adventures, the Birthday Group women have opened up their world.

These women are women of faith. They join hands before the meal, saying grace for God's generous gifts. For the gift of friendship. For the gift of Barbara's presence, and her continued strength in the midst of her battle with cancer. The women invoke the memory of the two group members who are now in God's hands: Frances, the group's founder, and Freda, who died three years ago. The women say their "amens," and then look up and smile at the framed photographs of their two friends that they have set at the table's end.

"They are with us even now. They are with us today," says Ann with conviction, without the slightest hint of irony. "Frances and Freda would love you. We will introduce you some day."

These women have been gathering in celebration for almost thirty years. They first met in 1972, when they were housewives in their twenties and thirties. With small children underfoot, they desperately needed time out of the house to breathe deeply. "You don't quite know what it's like to take care of little ones every day until you've done so yourself. I totally enjoyed being a mother, but you feel like you can never finish a sentence or a task, let alone have an intelligent thought," Nedra explains. The church offered them escape and first brought them together.

They say there's a church on every corner in Ada, Oklahoma. And a quick ride through town—ten minutes end to end—bears that out. A few Methodist, some Pentecostal, but mostly Southern Baptist. The Birthday Group women met at the Joy Bible Study class, titled "Jesus, Others and You," sponsored by the Ada First Baptist Church. The church had a nursery where they could drop off their kids. They would gather eagerly every Wednesday morning for several hours, and though they focused on Bible teachings, sometimes they would lay aside their studies and talk of more intimate matters. One of their rituals was to place names of loved ones in a basket in the center of the room, people in pain or somehow at risk, and together they would pray for them.

"We would prolong those mornings as long as we could," recalls Nedra, seated at the place of honor at the table's head. "We would find reasons to go out to lunch together before returning to our diapers and ironing, our cooking and daily routines. It was subtle how it took shape, but we found all of a sudden that we knew each other's birthdays," Nedra reminisces. "And even if it did not fall on a Wednesday study morning, we began meeting for birthday luncheons and taking small gifts. We found that we had become the closest of friends and wanted to celebrate together. That's really how the Birthday Group began."

Though the women share the bond of their faith, they represent a wonderful assortment of personalities and backgrounds, and they enjoy their differences. There is a spirit of openness about these women, whatever their first impressions of one another might have been.

"I'll never forget the morning at church when Kay and I first met, years and years ago," Ann fondly recalls. Relishing the memory, Kay jumps in. "I was sitting in Sunday school and this strange woman sits down next to me and just starts talking. I didn't know her at all," Kay says, throwing a mock-bewildered glance in Ann's direction. "She says to me, 'I have had the worst week. I got three tickets, two for running the same stop sign. And I ran over a mailbox. I was so embarrassed I made my husband, Jim, call the people to tell them I had done it. Then I went to the drive-in with the kids and didn't see the chain strung across the drive. I drove right through and broke it. Then I backed into a tree, and later the same day, when I got home, I ran into the garage wall.' And as Ann is saying all of this," Kay explains, "I'm moving my chair further and further away from her."

"That was the week when the State of Oklahoma sent me a letter saying that they wanted to rehabilitate me, I had gotten so many tickets," Ann interjects.

"When I got home from church that morning," Kay continues, finishing the story, "I told my husband, Gary, 'I just met the strangest woman in Sunday school.'"

"And when I got home," Ann echoes without missing a beat, "I told my husband that I had just met the coldest fish."

Ann and Kay became the best of friends. Their backyards now adjoin. Ann convinced her husband, Jim, to buy their house because it backed up to Kay's. She had imagined them meeting in their backyards in the morning for coffee, though, life being as hectic as it is, they never have.

There are obvious differences in style within the Birthday Group. Judy, dressed in her favorite attire of blue jeans, points to her friend Ann and observes, "This is *Dynasty*—and I'm *Little House on the Prairie.*" Ann indeed has a hint of glamour about her, in her white linen and pearls. But she pooh-poohs the thought, as if her elegance were all just a goof. One member displays the lack of concern about disparities in wealth. She relates to the women, with some measure of proud disdain, a story about her son's ex-girlfriend, a high-society gal. "I remember when I first met her she told me that her family was the Who's Who of her hometown. I told her we were the So Whats of Ada."

While, in many groups, inequality of resources might cause discomfort, or just the worry that they couldn't all afford the same sorts of fun, these women betray no jealousy or ill will toward the greater fortunes of some. The women give freely to one another and appreciate what each has to offer. "We have one member who is always sending cards, or buying small gifts for us and leaving them anonymously in our mailboxes," observes Nedra with affection. "And Ann is our gracious hostess. She is always opening her home to us for Christmas parties, pool parties, anniversary celebrations."

"When I die, I don't want to have anything left. I want to give it all away to my friends and family while I'm still alive," Ann says with a smile. Ann was born poor, the daughter of a welder, and she wouldn't mind leaving this good earth that way.

It is a simple concept, a birthday group. At the beginning of each year, the women draw names. The host decides when, where, and how to celebrate. As the women have come to know each other's personalities, the celebrations and gifts have become more creative and particular to the nature and fancy of the guest of honor.

Kay loved her fifty-third birthday celebration, when Nedra hosted. Nedra pulled her picnic table to a sandy, level spot in the dry creekbed that runs kitty-corner from her home. She brought in bales of hay and lit a glowing campfire. The table was decorated with a forest green cloth and fall leaves gathered from surrounding trees. An old camping lantern and a hurricane lamp lent their soft light to the falling dusk. "We told ghost stories and jokes, then had a songfest. We walked down the road together and returned to our coffee, perked over the slowly dying embers," Nedra recalls. "Even Mother Nature sent me a gift," Kay adds. "A full harvest moon."

Sue says, "My most memorable birthday was when I turned forty. Early that morning the doorbell rang. When I opened the door, I found Ann and Kay singing a dirgelike version of Happy Birthday. Those ornery ladies had hung strange-looking decorations on the tree in front of my house." Hanging from various limbs were a bedpan, a walker, a cane, and other items from Kay and Gary's rest home. Kay and her husband own a chain of nursing homes. Sue laughs. "They were helping me advance gracefully into middle age."

Later that day, the group gathered at a local Mexican restaurant for lunch. The day had turned rainy, and during lunch, a very fine-looking young man in a raincoat walked up to their table. "Before you could say 'Jack Robinson,'" Sue continues, "he was taking off his raincoat to reveal a teeny, tiny bright red Speedo."

"And your face turned the same color," Nedra grins.

With so many birthdays celebrated, the group has evolved and become an integral part of the women's lives. In the early years, the women helped pull each

Barbara (with masked friend)

other through the travails of young motherhood. "I remember when Sue's son, Scott, was born," Nedra recalls. "Sue went into labor prematurely, and things were pretty much touch and go for a while there." When the women of the Birthday Group were called with the news, they assembled immediately in the hospital waiting room, and spent several harrowing hours on their knees deep in prayer. "Scott weighed just over four pounds when he was born, but God protected him. We will always have a soft spot in our hearts for Scott," Nedra comments. "You can see the gentle spirit in his eyes.

"It's funny, we first met as young mothers," Nedra wistfully recalls. "And now we talk about our children's weddings and the births of our grandchildren."

Getting ready for their children's weddings has been such a special time for this group. "I remember," Sue says, "for one of the kids' showers, we all got together at Ann's house to make homemade tarts. We were gathered in Ann's kitchen, rolling out the pastry dough, covered with flour and looking like ghosts. We formed an assembly line to place the fruit on top. First peach slices, then kiwi, then raspberries. Ann kept cracking the whip, yelling at our slow pace. 'Come on, Judy, you're too slow. Kay has already made five tarts to your two.'"

In a town as small as Ada, there are no secrets. Friendships depend upon acceptance, discretion, and forgiveness. There is a distinct sense that the four corners of Ada may not always have been quite large enough to contain these women's dreams and aspirations. "We weren't all as contented when we started out here," admits Ann. "I did that for so long in my life, wanting something more. I wanted to live in New York City. For a time, I wanted to go to law school. I spent a lot of time in this group, pouring out my frustrations, my dreams for a bigger life."

Ann pauses a moment, caught in thought. "We all know women who have left Ada. Who have left their children, their families, in search of a larger life. But as you age, you get wiser. This group has helped me realize that you have everything you need right here in front of you. That you can grow and be happy without sacrificing someone in order to do it."

"As you age, you get wiser. This group has helped me realize that you have everything you need right here in front of you. That you can grow and be happy without sacrificing someone in order to do it."

For many, the Birthday Group has strengthened marriages. The Birthday Group, it seems, has been a stabilizing element in these women's lives. It is the place where the women have exposed their frustrations, their disappointments, their moments of doubt. "Men and women are different," Nedra observes.

"Sometimes we need an outlet, a place where we can say what we want. We let each other have our pity parties. Good thing we never have them all on the same day."

"We laughed not too long ago," Nedra reflects, "about the hundreds of years we have all been married. It is pretty remarkable. All of us have been married to our original husbands for thirty to forty years." Nedra smiles mischievously as she looks around the room. "Give or take a husband or two."

The women of the Birthday Group describe themselves as a sisterhood. Their siblinglike connection may come from the fact that few have sisters of their own. Only Nedra didn't grow up surrounded by boys. She considers herself lucky to be blessed with her sister, LaDonna, who is in attendance at Nedra's birthday celebration.

"Tell us about your childhood, Nedra," Kay says softly, focusing the attention squarely on the guest of honor. Kay knows that Nedra loves to tell a story. "We want to hear all about what it was like to grow up with a sister."

"LaDonna and I had a childhood full of adventures that have cemented us for life," Nedra responds. Their father was also a welder, and quite expert in his craft. Each summer, he would take on special projects, working on oil pipelines throughout the country. The family went on three-month jaunts far beyond the Oklahoma borders.

"I remember coming home from Washington State," Nedra continues. "We had a beautiful 1955 Buick Century hardtop, light blue and white with a rolled and pleated white leather interior. We were driving through northern Colorado, crossing the Continental Divide. There was still snow on the ground. We had stopped to do Chinese fire drill, trading spots during the long ride. I was trading with Dad, taking his spot in the backseat, while he went up front to drive. Well, when I got out of the car, they just forgot me. Dad had just woken up and he drove off and left me at the side of the road, no socks, no shoes, in the snow." Nedra laughs out loud. "I remember seeing the taillights drive out of sight."

"And I slept through the whole thing," adds LaDonna.

"Do you remember coming home from Kentucky that next summer and stopping at Graceland?" LaDonna continues. "We saw Elvis, remember?"

"You saw Elvis?" Ann interrupts, her eyes widening.

"Yes, and of course I remember," says Nedra with appropriate gravity, answering sister and friend in turn. "I was seventeen. Elvis was twenty-five. He was such a foxy thing. So tan and beautiful, with a gleaming black duck tail haircut. He came down to the fence where a small group of us tourists had gathered. He was so nice. We asked him questions. One was what was his favorite drink. He said simply in his southern drawl, 'Buttermilk.'"

Finally, with great ceremony, the women present Nedra with her birthday cake, elaborately decorated and topped with dozens of flaming candles. They wish their friend well as she faces the sixtieth year of her life, and unveil their carefully chosen gifts: matching table lamps and a hand-painted birdhouse for Nedra's herb garden.

It is now two o'clock. Barbara quietly announces that she has to go; she needs to rest. She calls her husband, Jim, to collect her. Refusing their pleas of assistance, she makes her way slowly across the polished wooden floor, taking stiff, tentative steps, one following another.

"Barbara is a warrior," says Nedra with quiet admiration upon her friend's departure, "and an inspiration to all who know her." Barbara is now a ten-year cancer survivor, though her cancer has returned.

"When we found out about the recurrence of Barbara's illness," recounts Nedra, "we all tried to gather our wits. Each of us has tried to help out however we can. We take turns driving her to her chemotherapy and radiation treatments. We take food to her house. We communicate our love through our prayers. She is a living miracle." Sue smiles, recalling her friend's particular pleasures. "Barbara loves to shop for clothes. So once, when she was going through a really hard time, the group just snatched her out of her home by surprise and drove her down to Fort Worth. We tucked her into a wheelchair, and all shopped with her for hours. She just loved it.

"Now Barbara is back on her feet again," Sue observes. "She is going places with us again. She is making trips with her family. She was once so weak. I remember times when she was so nauseated from her chemotherapy that she couldn't even sit up. But she would always make it to our Birthday Group celebrations. Sometimes she would just lie down next to us, reaching a hand out to touch us. She just wanted to be near us. And we wanted to be near her."

"These women are a blessing," Kay says, her gentle voice clutched by emotion. "I remember when my dad died. I'm not sure how these women even found out, but by the time I got to my mom's house, they were all there. Every one of them." Nedra will be forever grateful for the women's abiding presence in the wake of her father's death. "I feel that I am who I am today knowing these women love me and care about what I am doing," Nedra reflects. "That knowledge not only strengthens me for the rough patches but gives me someone with whom to celebrate life."

The women lovingly remember one member, Frances, who ran the Bible study group where they met and who was the initial, informal leader of the group gatherings. "Frances was a beautiful person," Nedra recalls. "She knew the Scriptures backwards and forwards. We were in awe of her. She was short and round, with an impish smile and such a sharp wit, it would take you by surprise. Fannie was about ten or twelve years older than us, and we all looked up to her. She was very wise and taught us a great deal." Frances had breast cancer at the age of twenty-six, before the other women even knew her. She endured a double mastectomy while raising two small children. Then, in 1987, she was diagnosed with a malignant brain tumor, and after battling the illness for more than a year, passed away on September 3, 1988.

"I remember when the Birthday Group celebrated her last birthday,

January eighth," Nedra recalls. "Fannie had just gotten out of the hospital and was in a wheelchair at home. Her head was shaved and she had a fresh, shiny pink scar from the surgery. We were all gathered at her feet, and she was recounting funny stories and telling all of us how much she loved us. It hit us all so hard when Frances died. We were then in our mid- to late forties and the cold hand of death had reached out and touched us in a very personal way. We miss her so much."

Nedra takes a slow breath. "Frances really opened us up to the power of faith. She made us realize that our group bond was such a blessing, and a result of our deeper faith." The Birthday Group women speak often of God, but it is not so much religion as faith that binds these women. Nedra likes to say that as they get older they get less religious but more spiritual. In the face of huge pain and loss they call upon their faith, and endure not with bitterness but with resilience and grace. The women believe in the power of prayer, and in times of need, they will mobilize their "prayer chain." By telephone, the women will contact one another. And then, as a group, they will pray.

Sometimes it comes down to this. People whom you love die, and it is hard to let go. It is hard to lift your head above the wall of pain. Even these women, women of profound faith, know this to be true. In these raw moments, the women of the Birthday Group count on each other.

In 1997, the Birthday Group women buried yet another of their own. Freda, the baby of the group, discovered the day after her fifty-second birthday that she had advanced breast cancer. "She had never had a mammogram, never. If we had only known, we would have implored her to pay better attention to her own health. She went through chemotherapy, radiation, but it was simply too late," Nedra recalls quietly.

Freda continued to attend Birthday Group celebrations until weeks before her death. She was not in denial about her illness, and would talk freely about it with the other women. "I remember one day we just sat together and she wept and wept," Nedra recalls. "Then she apologized for it. The group was the one place she took her sorrow and fear. She didn't allow herself to do that often at home because it hurt her husband, Ron."

On October 9, 1997, one month and two days before her fifty-third birthday, Freda died. "Ron knew how close we all were," Nedra continues. "He wanted the Birthday Group to help in the preparation of her body. We all assembled at her home. And then we went to the funeral home together. We had to make sure that Freda looked just the way she would have wanted. Natural and beautiful. She had the most lovely complexion.

"Freda had borrowed a dress from Ann the previous July, for her nephew's wedding," Nedra explains. "A lovely, simple pink linen dress. She had been through so much by then, but she had looked gorgeous in it.

"We buried Freda in that dress," Nedra states.

"Freda took her time when she spoke. She spoke low and slow," Sue recalls with obvious fondness. "She had this funny habit of starting a conversation right in the middle of a thought. Half the time, it would take us a few minutes to figure out what she was talking about."

"At first," Ann explains, "we each individually thought it was just us."

"But then, at some point, we realized that was the way Freda spoke," adds Sue.

"We were teasing her one afternoon at my pool, remember?" Ann asks. The other women nod in amusement. "She was lying on a float in the water, just laughing and laughing about it."

Barbara and Nedra, Sue and Judy, Ann and Kay, and all of the other women of the Birthday Group are bound by a sense of faith that allows them to see the mysterious beauty in all aspects of life. Even when life involves transitioning through hardship, illness, and death. The women have a tradition, unbroken for

clockwise from lower right: Barbara, Judy, Nedra, Kay, Sue, Ann

many years, of having their photograph taken during the Christmas holidays. Ann gives a framed copy to each of the women as a gift. Five years back, right after Barbara had lost all of her hair to the ravages of chemotherapy, she had hesitated at sitting for the photo. Ann took charge and adroitly turned the situation on its head. "We're all going to wear hats. That way we can all look as good as Barbara."

The holiday photograph from 1995 shows a group of broadly smiling women, gathered around the gracefully winding staircase in Ann's home. They are all in hats. Barbara stands in the front row, third from the right, adorned in a wide-brimmed hat with an extravagant feather plume jutting high above the crown. She is beaming.

"Perhaps it took the dying of our friends to realize what we have created," Nedra says in quiet reflection. "As we have aged and hopefully become wiser, we realize what a special gift we have been given. This is no ordinary friendship. The people around us, our children, all grown now, comment on the uniqueness of our bond. My grandmother and mother have a saying. 'A burden shared is a burden eased.' I add to that, 'A joy shared is a joy magnified.'"

"Perhaps it took the dying of our friends to realize what we have created. As we have aged and hopefully become wiser, we realize what a special gift we have been given."

From such a simple beginning, celebrating birthdays with the same circle of friends, these women have created a bond that will keep them together year after year, for as long as they are alive.

The women now each wear a delicate gold bracelet, graced with a single, tiny bell. When they hear the bell ring, they think of each other. And they pray.

conclusion

how to bring a women's group into your life
or rejuvenate one that is dear to your heart

Perhaps you've decided to introduce a women's group into your life, or are part of a women's group that is looking for a new approach. In this final chapter, we offer wisdom derived from our experience interviewing women's groups all over the country. Their stories have moved both of us to add new dimensions to our own women's groups, and it's our hope that you, too, will be inspired. We have found that a certain level of intention is valuable in creating and sustaining an enduring group bond.

There is no set formula for forming or joining a women's group. While many groups focus on women's spirituality and ritual, or on learning, many others come together just for fun. As the Bridgies taught us, the strongest bonds can develop through something as simple as a weekly game of bridge. We did, however, discover a wonderful range of activities through which groups have strengthened their ties, and we will share some of our favorites.

SO YOU WANT A WOMEN'S GROUP

You like the idea of a sustained and formal commitment to a group of friends and are willing to invest the time and emotion. First, consider carefully what you really want. Truthfully assess your needs and desires, and the amount of time and energy you are willing to commit. Also reflect on your past experiences with any women's groups you might have been a part of, and talk with anyone you know who is in a group. Ask yourself, do you want to join an existing group, or start a new one? Do you want fun, study, ritual, intimacy, or companionship in a new venture? We know many women who have joined a book group only to realize that they really were seeking a group with stronger personal connections.

SHOULD YOU JOIN AN EXISTING GROUP OR START YOUR OWN?

Existing groups—those that are open to new members—offer the ease of a ready-made structure and a depth of experience. Joining such a group may provide just the sense of comfort and connection you seek. But there may also be discomfort in finding your place in an established group, and in responding to the group's and your own expectations of intimacy. Many women have told us that the most successful way to join a group is to have at least one member who is already a close friend.

While starting your own group may seem daunting, it also presents great opportunity. You can influence the group's style, its purpose, the frequency of meetings, the level of commitment required, the type of activity it is centered around. You can also identify the women with whom you want to spend time.

FIND A CO-CREATOR

You may find it more satisfying and less intimidating to start a group with another woman. A partner can help overcome self-doubt, that nagging fear of throwing a dinner party to which no one comes. The synergy between you will also generate fresh ideas, broaden your sense of possibility, and ultimately help sharpen your focus. A co-creator will also help to expand the circle of women you can invite, and provide greater potential resources, contacts and connections.

Barbara formed her group eighteen years ago with her friend Judi, in the wake of Barbara's break-up with the boyfriend who had originally brought them together. With Judi's encouragement—"Let's just do it without the guys"—they invited other women and formalized a friendship that might otherwise have faded.

THE PEOPLE YOU INVITE MAY MATTER MORE THAN YOU WOULD IMAGINE

The selection of women you invite is a critical decision and one that is not easy to undo. Groups persevere for years with the mistake of having invited someone who is not a good fit, because the rule, whether spoken or unspoken, in most groups is that once invited, a member cannot be asked to leave. The choice may seem obvious. Your initial instincts may be to invite your best friend, a co-worker, or a new neighbor. But do not invite out of a sense of obligation. Think hard before you ask.

Also be clear in your intentions and priorities. Ask yourself whether you want to see more of friends you already have or are really looking to forge new friendships. If you mostly want to spend more time with current friends, then you should include them in your decision-making about how to formalize a group. If you are intent on pursuing a particular activity in your group, such as yoga, then you must be sure you invite people who have a genuine interest.

In issuing invitations, also think about each woman's style and how the set of women will mesh as a group. Consider whether certain women might be dominating, or whether they might be unwilling to open up or to respect boundaries. We've learned that just one woman's unwillingness to be intimate inhibits the entire group. Many women we've talked with admit that the harsh or judgmental comment of a single member has made them want to leave their group. An environment of safety, free of judgment, is essential.

Personal histories matter. Consider the impact individual friendships may have on the larger group. Preexisting friendships may be perceived as cliquish or make others feel excluded. Unresolved conflict between friends may emerge. While the Company of Women in Atlanta was able to confront early conflict between two members, many groups faced with such a challenge would simply dissolve.

Decide whether you want diversity or homogeneity, and to what degree. Don't seek out diversity for diversity's sake. Many find security and a sense of belonging in gathering with women who are similar to them. The Crew in Chicago are firmly bound by their common experiences as high-achieving black professionals. Our own Washington, D.C., group is relatively homogeneous, all middle-class women of a similar age. Over the years, however, we have decided to include women who mirror the changing life circumstances of members in the group. We have assured that stay-at-home moms and career women, the married and the single, all have another member who shares those experiences. In contrast, the Company of Women thrives on wider diversity. Their ages range from thirty-five to sixty-five, they are gay and straight, married and divorced, well off and from more modest means.

When making your selection:

❧ Think before you ask.

❧ Don't invite out of obligation.

- Consider personal style, personal histories, and preexisting friendships.

- Decide on a degree of diversity.

GATHERING YOUR GROUP

One of the easiest ways to get a group going is to start with a natural circle of friends, or start with a core group and have each woman invite another friend. But we've heard stories of successful groups forming from a group of women who've only met briefly before. The founder of Chicks 'n' Flicks, Robin, started the group with a number of women she'd met at an international women's film festival. She didn't want to lose touch, so she invited them all over for dinner and the group took off from there.

ACCEPTING NEW MEMBERS

While most groups we talked to have closed membership, a few offer open invitations to new members. The Yoga Circle has thrived for more than thirty years and is open to anyone who wants to show up for an evening. One thing is for sure: if you are going to invite new members, you should always get the entire group's approval before you ask a new person if she's interested. Not checking in advance can lead to hurt feelings and hampered friendships if the expected invitation never arrives.

In the end, go with your intuition when deciding who to invite into your women's group. Closed for many years to new members, the Fabulous Group invited Beth to join just because "it felt right." And it worked.

Closed membership certainly seems to engender stronger bonds. Most groups we met were closed to new members, finding a stable configuration of women essential to group trust, intimacy, and longevity. Our Washington, D.C., group has only added new members to replace those who have moved away. We have noticed that even when each member is enthusiastic about the new person, it nonetheless changes the group dynamic and requires a period of readjustment.

If your group is action-oriented, however, open membership may allow for an ongoing injection of new energy and influences.

CONSIDER THE SIZE OF THE GROUP CAREFULLY

The number of women can affect the level of intimacy. Groups seem to work best with between five and twelve members. But the optimal size should also be determined in part based on the group's intention. If your aim is more action oriented—study, social activism, fund-raising—a larger group may be preferable, because members can offer diverse resources and more easily share the responsibilities. (GNO)2 of New Orleans, intent on having fun, sought twelve members so that each one could plan a monthly adventure. If your intention is a more personal one, a dozen women could be challenging. For example, many groups have some form of "check-in" at each meeting, where members share what's been happening in their lives. With too many members, this kind of ritualized sharing could take a prohibitive amount of time.

That said, also keep in mind that a group of a certain size can help to take the pressure off certain friendships within a group, allowing tensions between members to be diffused rather than to become the focus of get-togethers.

EARLY ENDEAVORS

The early meetings may feel a bit unnerving, and one way to ease the strain of expectations, particularly those of immediate intimacy, is to convene around an activity, or a theme or intention that captivates interest. Over time, your group will begin to feel closer and you will find your own unique ways to share the more personal.

Here are some ideas for early endeavors:

- Begin with a ritual that reveals. Engage in a candle-lighting ceremony, such as that created by the Rosh Chodesh group of Philadelphia. One woman begins by lighting her candle and reciting her matrilineal heritage. She then lights the candle of the woman seated beside her, and each woman follows in turn. Once the circle is closed, you can bring others "into the circle" symbolically, offering words of encouragement or remembrance. "I would like to bring my mother into the circle. She is starting a new career at age sixty-five and is feeling a bit uncertain."

- Approach your first gathering with humor; make it light and campy. Remember that at their initial dinner, (GNO)2 had party games and a gag gift for everyone. Laughter causes people to let their guard down.

- Meet around an activity. Learn a new game or skill together. The Mah-jongg Girls focused their early meetings on learning the game with the assistance of their mothers. Others have played bridge, learned yoga, or simply gone to the movies.

- Study together. Select a discussion topic, or an article or book to read. You might even want to circulate questions in advance of the meeting to allow time for reflection and to provoke a more substantive conversation.

- Relate the details of your life. Storytelling is an age-old tradition among women, and we are good at it. Absorbing personal histories will enhance your understanding of one another and make you more aware and sensitive of one another's dreams and desires.

WHEN IN DOUBT, EAT

The universal language of women's groups is food. Almost without exception, the groups we met take advantage of the joys of group meals as a sure means of connecting.

Here are a few culinary suggestions:

- Go out to dinner. Try a different restaurant each time and get to know hot new spots in your area. This is also a great way of gathering for women who don't like to cook!

- Serve food based on a theme. A New Orleans book group serves dessert each time they meet. When reading a book on Vietnam, the hostess drove to a Vietnamese market in Eastern New Orleans and bought the appropriate pastries. The standard was set; each month's hostess must now match her dessert to the book being read.

- Cook for each other. For almost twenty years, our women's group in Washington, D.C., has taken turns experimenting with new recipes. Every member says she learned to cook by making dinner for the group.

- Cook together. For years, a group of Santa Fe women has convened in one another's kitchens, working together on recipes from around the world.

- Now to counter the effects of all this eating, go to a spa together! One group in San Francisco goes on a spa outing once a year—this year in Italy.

NOTED ON THE ROAD

Our visits across America opened our eyes to the breadth of experience among women's groups. As we learned about new ideas, we introduced many into our own group in Washington, D.C. We hope the following selection of creative approaches will be inspiring to you as well.

Girls Just Want to Have Fun

Use your women's group as a license to play. As our chapters suggest...

- Close down a beauty salon, bring the champagne, and drink your way through manicures and pedicures.

- See and review movies together. The busy women of Chicks 'n' Flicks didn't have time to read a book every month, but knew they could manage a movie. Their potluck dinners are based on the movie's theme.

- Take an intensive course together to acquire a fun skill. Tennis camp, a yoga retreat, wind surfing, skiing lessons, knitting. A group of women in Los Angeles, who have been meeting for years, impulsively decided to go to surfing school together.

- Ride motorcycles. If you don't know how, take lessons together.

- Shop as a pack—The Alpha Chis of Indiana travel to New York City each year to shop; the only time they visited a museum, they stayed far from the art and close to the museum shop. And the Phenomenal Ladies Motorcycle Club of Maryland never takes a ride without bungee cords for the shopping bags acquired on the road.

- Go to the racetrack on opening day together like (GNO)2. Winner buys lunch.

- Travel together. The Alpha Chis, now scattered across several states, take an annual vacation together. The Dallas Once-a-Year Getaway Group does the same. If some members are less able to afford these adventures, pool your resources and subsidize!

- Play bridge or poker. Over monthly games of buanco, a group of women in Seattle have become one another's closest friends. In Hollywood, a group of struggling actresses plays Truth or Dare over pitchers of margaritas. The deepest of truths are revealed, and the dares push the women forward in their careers.

- Have a slumber party. Put on your pj's, bring your favorite pillow, and talk through the night.

- Play matching games. The Rosh Chodesh women periodically share "the table of contents of their life"—baby pictures, journal entries from the teen years, photos of old boyfriends; the other group members are put to the test of guessing whose life is on the table.

Reminisce

One of the best ways to bond with other women is to reveal the details of your lives.

- Tell each other your life stories. The Rosh Chodesh women began at an annual retreat. The stories were so rich that they decided to continue over many future gatherings until each story was fully told. Revisit your stories as your group bond deepens. New facets and revelations will emerge.

- As a group, share your greatest regrets. Examining these disappointments within the support of the group may help a woman change her future course. The Company of Women has moved many of its members toward their dreams: artistry, financial independence, homes by the ocean.

- Pay tribute to your mothers. Talk about your relationships with your mothers, how you are like them and how that makes you feel. Go around the circle and recite, "My mother loves…'A well-cut suit, romance novels, giving her young grandsons a warm bath. Walks in nature, the written word, Cajun dancing.'" Both the quiet rhythm of this exercise and its revelations mesmerized our Washington, D.C., group.

Live Life Events

- Rally in the face of a member's life challenges: illness, death, divorce. Many women's groups organize meals, child care, or deal with the logistics of lawyers and therapists. Deborah of Rosh Chodesh will never forget how the group cared for her family during her bout with cancer. They played with her children so that she could simply sit on her couch and deal with her chemotherapy. (GNO)2 hosted a "kick-off lunch" before Linda's surgery. "It was like the group huddle before the game."

- Honor pregnancy as well as birth. The Study Group held "Blessing Ways" for the expectant mothers, massaging bodies, lighting candles, and offering wishes for new life.

- Create wedding rituals. The Fabulous Group from the Bay Area began a tradition of inviting all of the women at the wedding to participate in a pre-ceremony ritual. They sang and danced, forming a tight spiral around the mother and bride.

〜 Celebrate birthdays. The Birthday Group draws names from a hat each year, then organizes a celebration and gift for each member. The Mahjongg Girls tailor their birthday celebrations to each woman's interests and passions; Lauren, lover of Latin culture, was treated to an evening of tapas and salsa.

Immerse Yourself in Intellectual Thought

〜 Create your own salon. For more than 140 years, the Discussion Group of Sandy Springs, Maryland, has charged its members to bring to the monthly meeting "one question and one comment" about the world or current events. They have kept meeting minutes of their discussions, which date back to the Civil War.

〜 Examine a topic of importance to your lives. The Network came together when the women were entering their sixties to learn about health and aging. Confronting mid-life change, a women's group that had been meeting for twenty years on Quadras Island, British Columbia, spent a year studying and discussing menopause.

〜 Invite guest speakers to your book or study group. The Tuesday Discussion Group of New Orleans, which has been meeting since 1952, taps into the Tulane University faculty.

〜 Organize a forum for the larger community on an issue of interest to your group. The Study Group began in the 1980s by holding lectures on nonviolence and nuclear disarmament.

〜 Read aloud together. The Northhampton Book Club has been meeting for over a century in western Massachusetts for oral readings and tea. And a women's drama group reads plays aloud.

Do Good, Change the World

- ❧ Fund-raise. The loss of a mother to breast cancer has caused three sisters to form a women's group around fund-raising for breast cancer research. This bicoastal group—with separate circles in Los Angeles and New York City—has bonded around their preparation for annual fund-raising galas, which have raised millions of dollars to date.

- ❧ Volunteer together. Viewing their joint philanthropy as being a bit removed from real life, a group of Hollywood screenwriters began working personally with disadvantaged kids in the Los Angeles public school system.

- ❧ Build bridges through shared experience. In Baltimore, Maryland, a multiracial group of women meets on the first Saturday of every month. Over their own individual craft projects and ordered-in lunch, the group seeks to combat racism.

- ❧ Save the earth. Enjoy the outdoors. The Grand Old Broads of the Wilderness hike and camp in the Rockies and engage in advocacy and fund-raising on behalf of the environment.

- ❧ Take on an annual project. The Mah-jongg Girls participate in an AIDS walk. (GNO)2 selects a different charity every year: gathering holiday gifts for kids with HIV/AIDS, raising funds for a girls' sports scholarship.

A Circle Unbroken

- ❧ Honor the women of all generations in your life.

- ❧ Like the Rosh Chodesh women, recite your matrilineal heritage at the outset of every meeting.

- Bring your family heirlooms to the group table. Each woman in the Tea Group sips from her grandmother's teacup at their gatherings.

- Form a mother-daughter book group. A group in Seattle, Washington, asked their daughters for suggestions of girls to invite, to ensure their comfort.

- Introduce your daughters to your women's group. The Rosh Chodesh group celebrates the bat mitzvah of each daughter with blessings and small, symbolic gifts: a jade heart-shaped pendant—"go with your heart"; a tiny straw basket—"be open and fill up." The Detroit Study Group celebrated one daughter's menstruation by sharing their own stories of this life change.

- Pass it on. Several women in the Tuesday Discussion Group invited their daughters to join the group at the time of their marriage.

Lead with the Creative

Use your women's group to make time for creativity. Use its support to fight inhibition.

- Let a teacher provide inspiration. The Muses of Washington, D.C., hire a teacher every season to instruct them in the "art of the unconscious." They have gotten to know one another over time by painting together. They have progressed from painting Christmas cards to producing an art show. The proceeds will go to a charity of choice.

- Create objects for your own group rituals. The candlesticks and "shmatas" used in the candle-lighting ritual of the Rosh Chodesh group were made by hand at their retreat.

↩ Use your group meetings as a source of creative discipline. One group of Philadelphia women meets weekly in the early-morning hours to engage in creative writing exercises based on Julia Cameron's *The Artist's Way*. One woman is now publishing her first book.

↩ Use your group resources to get ahead together. The Tea Group of Boston not only reviews and critiques each other's artwork but organizes and produces group shows.

Harness Technology

↩ Connect electronically—consider meeting virtually. The Spirit Group, in and around Washington, D.C., meets on-line to talk about work and life. Their bonds have transcended cyberspace; when one woman's mother died, everyone showed up at the funeral, meeting one another face-to-face for the first time.

↩ Reach out to the global community of women. The Boston Tea Group has created a Web site and is developing plans for a "global tea."

Push the Edges of the Envelope

Use the safety of your women's group to take on a challenging or unlikely activity, or to examine facets of yourself you might never explore on your own.

↩ Share your fantasies or thoughts of who you were in a former life.

↩ Conduct an "angel walk," like Rosh Chodesh. Form two parallel lines. Have each woman walk slowly through the center, eyes closed, while you caress her face and shoulders. Whisper affirmations into her ear, wonderful things about her. "It was profound. It was as if it did not occur in real time."

꿈 Explore your alter ego or your secret longings for a different identity. A group of Alaska women assumes a different thematic disguise every time they meet. The women get to experience in public what it is like to be blond, an older woman, even a man.

꿈 Shed your inhibitions and your clothes. The Bridgies, a bunch of Yankee women, have been known to skinny-dip together, to the hosting member's chagrin. And our D.C. women's group, inspired by *The Ladies of Rylstone*, spontaneously shed their bras and blouses and ate their dinner bare-breasted in their pearls.

꿈 Use angel cards—available at many bookstores—as a means of assessing the past and contemplating the future. The Yoga Circle meets on New Year's Day to draw three cards and to reflect on those drawn the previous year, i.e., *Courage, Power, Transformation; Beauty, Gratitude, Intuition.*

꿈 Observe the change of seasons with ritual. The Bay Area Fabulous Group celebrates the winter solstice with a bonfire on the beach. They cast off the burdens and disappointments of the past year by writing them on paper and setting them on fire. Their spring rites include the resurrection of a maypole, adorned with fresh flowers and ribbons.

꿈 Begin your gathering with a centering exercise. The Yoga Circle chants to shed the stresses of the day. The Mother of All Women's Groups, on Quadras Island, British Columbia, begins each meeting with a meditation around the compass points. North, south, east, west, and center. Many other groups similarly "call in the directions," drawing on both wiccan and Native American tradition.

Retreat

Take time away, together, from everyday life.

- ᴖ Create a sense of history and place. Each March, (GNO)2 returns to Thornwell, a member's family farm in west Louisiana. There they slow down and simply play: a Saturday-afternoon crawfish boil, a walk along the rim of the rice fields, hours hunched over a thousand-piece jigsaw puzzle.

- ᴖ Use your annual retreat to assess the focus of your group and to plan for the following year. Every October, the Rosh Chodesh women rent a house on the beach where they spend Saturday evening reviewing whether the past year's gatherings have met each member's needs, and mapping out the next year with intention.

- ᴖ See the world together. The Hens of Chicago rented an Airstream and journeyed through the American South. The Bridgies, in their sixties, have begun to travel together. Africa, Alaska—they are working their way through the alphabet.

LISTEN TO YOUR GROUP'S RHYTHM— HOW OFTEN DO YOU MEET?

What matters most about how often you meet is that your group approach the issue with intention and ongoing flexibility. The frequency and timing of gatherings should not become a burden or an obligation that members cannot honor. The interruptions of late arrivals or early departures can be painful and disrespectful to those who are present and fully participating. It is therefore important to set meeting times that allow women to stay through the group's close. If women are consistently missing your group meetings, perhaps you need to newly address your schedule.

Different groups thrive on different meeting schedules. The Company of Women meets only once a quarter, but for a weekendlong retreat. The Crew meets every Friday night for dinner; the women all like the set time because it is something they can count on in their busy lives. The Fabulous Group spent their first three years meeting every week. As they later noted a waning commitment to the group, they reassessed. With increasing family obligations, the women agreed to meet only twice a month—resulting in renewed commitment to the group.

In both setting a meeting date and in rescheduling one, some groups have adopted a quorum rule to prevent hurt feelings. If a predetermined number of members is able to meet, the meeting is a "go," no questions asked.

Determine with intention how often you want to meet. But remain flexible.

WHERE TO FIND YOURSELVES

Consider whether to meet in the same space every time, or to rotate—through one another's homes, different restaurants, or beautiful outdoor venues. It is a matter of sharing the burden versus establishing predictability.

GROUP DISCIPLINE: LESSONS FROM OUR TRAVELS

Women's groups vary greatly in their degree of formality and organization. It might be useful to discuss, and perhaps establish, ground rules as you begin. Consider the following issues and suggestions:

- *Leadership:* Does your group want to designate a leader/facilitator or to share leadership, in rotation or in pairs? Or should there be no leader at all? For years, the Yoga Circle had a formal leader; when she fell ill and could no longer lead, the group decided to proceed without one. The Rosh Chodesh group has no formal leader. Yet when engaged in study, it often defers to a few women with the greater depth of knowledge, who will prepare readings and exercises for the entire group.

- ✍ *Decision making:* How will decisions be made? By majority vote or consensus? The Chicks 'n' Flicks aim for consensus when choosing their flick, but will, when necessary, put the issue to a vote.

- ✍ *Following an established, ritualized process:* Should your group follow a set process at each meeting, or a ritual for opening and closing the group meeting?

- ✍ *Centering:* Our experience has taught us that generally some sort of "centering" exercise helps women move from casual conversation to attentive focus—if the group members are all accepting and comfortable with that approach. The centering can be as simple as lighting candles, singing a song, or quietly visualizing a center. The Muses of Washington, D.C., start each art session with a narrated meditation. The Fabulous Group begins each meeting by standing in a circle, hands linked, and grounding—literally feeling for the earth beneath their feet. They call in the directions, invoking the earth elements to achieve a deeper sense of group connection. The Birthday Group begins with a prayer.

- ✍ *Check-in:* If your group desires a certain level of intimacy, it may consider a formal check-in. To ensure that everyone gets their say, the Study Group uses a three-minute egg timer. The Company of Women, in contrast, allows every woman to speak as long as she desires. The Mother-Daughter Book Group passes around a "talking stick," decorated by the girls. The intention is to ensure that when one person holds the object and speaks, she will not be interrupted.

~ *Closing:* The closing of a meeting may be ritualized as well, to mark the ending of that evening's commitment. Rosh Chodesh closes every meeting with a song, and the blowing out of candles.

~ *Extending your community:* As your group develops more respect for its own importance, it may want to be a public part of life events and family ritual, and to share with others the community it has created. At weddings, bar and bat mitzvahs, funerals, many groups participate in the ritual as a group. They may offer blessings, song, or assistance. One of the most profound wedding memories of the Fabulous Group women is the spiral dance around the mother and bride, which engaged all of the women present. The Birthday Group of Ada helped prepare the body of one member who died; members spoke of their group friendship at the memorial service. Many groups invite family members to annual events. For the Rosh Chodesh women, it's their Fourth of July picnic; for the Fabulous Group it's their celebration of the winter solstice. And the Yoga Circle invites family to the Angel Party on New Year's Day.

~ *Lists and List-serves:* Many groups keep a list with contact information and the names and birthdays of husbands, partners, and children. And now they establish e-mail list-serves to help coordinate group events.

CREATING YOUR OWN HISTORY

Many groups, years later, have turned back and wished that they had documented their history. Five years along, the Fabulous Group realized they had never taken a group photo. Capture your time together, create a group archive. Here are some ideas:

The Visual: One member of the Birthday Group has a professional photo taken of the group every Christmas; it is her gift to all the members. The Bridgies keep a photo album of their antics over the years. The Tea Group has videotaped several of its group meetings. One member of (GNO)2 is the group archivist; she has years of photos and creates group collages.

The Written Word: Several members of the Rosh Chodesh group carefully document group gatherings in a journal. They tuck between its pages mementos of their rituals. (GNO)2 also keeps a journal; theirs is a bit more lighthearted, with hand-drawn diagrams of the beach houses and hotels where the group has stayed. A few members of the Bridgies have penned poems about the group; each member hangs a copy in her home.

Creativity: Chicks 'n' Flicks, (GNO)2, and many other groups save the creative invitations they design. One of the Bridgies created a monoprint with the assistance of her artist daughter in appreciation of her group's thirty years together. And the Tea Group pieced together a Tea Quilt, stored carefully and hung at all their art shows.

LEAVING LOVINGLY

Few groups are lucky enough to have their members stay forever. For whatever reason someone leaves, it is important to recognize that it will alter the group dynamic and may cause feelings of grief or even betrayal. How the leavetaking is handled—by both the group and the departing member—may determine the level of turmoil that ensues.

Several groups we have met have been shaken by having had members simply leave without a formal good-bye. And those tender feelings persist for many years. If someone leaves for lack of a good fit, it is worth talking as a group about the experience, and learning from it.

When women leave reluctantly—because of changed life circumstances—the departure should be acknowledged. Having learned from an earlier unmarked departure, the Fabulous Group had a celebration for the member who later moved away. The group both honored the woman's unique contributions and wished her well in her future life. She has since made many surprise return visits and is always welcomed. When one member moved to New York City, our Washington, D.C., group had a party where we presented her with handmade "vouchers"—good for an unlimited stay in each of our homes. For another departing member, we created a play spoofing her life and our group's role in it, which was videotaped and mailed to her.

Our Washington, D.C., group has also found comfort in the privilege of lifetime membership—once a member, always a member. Several women have moved away for a period of time, knowing that there would always be "group" to come home to, as visitors or upon their permanent return.

A BEND IN THE ROAD

Relationships within a women's group are not orderly. The very nature of a group—its conditions of vulnerability and exposure, as well as its long-term commitment—increases the possibility that things may not always go smoothly. The potential challenges are myriad: conflict among group members, broken trust, lack of openness, confidence betrayed, a judgmental or dominating voice.

Such problems should not be ignored. The women in this book teach us that *the key to tackling challenge is honesty, courage, and respectful directness.*

REVITALIZING YOUR GROUP—OR DISBANDING WITH LOVE

Perhaps the most frightening situation a group can face is one of stagnation and waning commitment. It is like silence in a marriage. While the group relationship, unattended, can disintegrate, we have seen many examples of the potential for rejuvenation.

The women of the Fabulous Group discussed their needs in light of their changed life circumstances. They decided to meet less frequently and to restructure their group process. They took care in drafting a formal document, The Seven Tenets of Commitment, which they signed in the presence of their families at a ceremony on the winter solstice.

Facing a sense of stagnation in our own Washington, D.C., women's group, our response was less formal but of equal impact. After seventeen years we introduced our first ritual—a centering exercise—and began a more structured approach. While we continue to cook for one another, we assign two other members the task of selecting a topic or article, circulating questions in advance, and leading the group discussion. Each woman speaks in turn, and no one interrupts.

Sometimes the problem is no deeper than restlessness and boredom. In responding to your group's mid-life crisis, consider the various ideas and approaches we noted on the road.

It is wise to acknowledge that some groups will not last forever. Celebrate the time the group was together, the friendships that were made, the memories you will always cherish. Don't feel as though it was a failure because you couldn't make enough adjustments to keep it going. One friend was in a "mom's group" that ended after many years. She recalls the experience fondly and says, "I like the notion of celebrating the years we had, rather than lamenting that they are over. Some of the members are missing out on some of the best memories because they are mourning the fact that we disbanded."

- Transform waning interest into renewed commitment.

- Consider introducing new ritual or a new approach.

- Disband in celebration.

ACCEPTING CHANGE AND APPRECIATING DIFFERENCE

The most successful and long-lived of groups remain accepting and open to change. As women age and enter different stages of life, what they want from their group changes as well. To remain vital, groups must be ever willing to reassess their approach.

The Study Group began with a rigorously intellectual focus and with no intention to explore the personal. Yet when a single member openly acknowledged the closeness that had developed among them and vocalized a broadly held desire to spend time on the personal, the group responded. They developed a three-minute check-in and later delved deeply into women's spirituality and ritual.

Rosh Chodesh has shifted its focus annually from learning to the personal, and back again, in response to members' voiced desires. Some years it has fully set aside its focus on learning because of the women's needs to tend to the personal.

Our agent, Gail Ross, wisely observes that when women become intensely bonded they serve as both a window to and a reflection of one another's lives. While many groups begin with a strong sense of sameness, their lives may later diverge. Change can be threatening. It can raise feelings of fear, jealousy, or conflict: career versus stay-at-home mom; success versus stagnation; children versus the choice not to have kids or infertility; marriage versus divorce. The continued strength of a women's group often turns on the willingness of its members to look inward and not be threatened by difference. Barbara's separation and divorce raised complicated emotions within our Washington, D.C., group, unexpected on all fronts. Several women, happily married, acknowledged a sense of unease in the face of the changes in Barbara's life. By openly discussing the layers of feeling, with the passage of time, our group was able to transcend these difficult moments.

Accepting change includes recognizing that over time friendships may shift;

individual levels of commitment and sense of belonging may waver. While the larger tensions may need to be addressed, there is a wisdom in appreciating the ebb and flow of any group dynamic. Remaining open returns you to a sense of commitment.

In our women's groups, we step outside the day-to-day of our lives and savor experiences and connections that are broader and richer. As Brenda Trivette of (GNO)2 observes, *"I go to my women's group as if to a feast."*

about the authors

Barbara Camens is an attorney in her own firm, Barr & Camens, in Washington, D.C., and is general counsel to an international union of newspaper journalists.

Tamara Kreinin is President and CEO of SIECUS (Sexuality Information and Education Council of the United States), a nonprofit organization located in New York City.

The authors are close friends and are both long-standing members of women's groups.